THE KING OF GLORY
AND THE
NATIONS OF THE WORLD

THE KING OF GLORY
AND THE
NATIONS OF THE WORLD

THE STORY OF MANKIND

ALON BARUCH

Ordering Information:

For orders and inquiries, please contact:
1-888-404-1388
www.goldtouchpress.com
book.orders@goldtouchpress.com

Printed in the United States of America

CONTENTS

DEDICATION

This book is dedicated to the King of glory, who is my source and savior and the true governor of the nations of the world. He alone has the solution to the problem of race and racism in the world today.

"The earth is the LORD's, and the fulness thereof;
the world, and they that dwell therein.
2. For he hath founded it upon the seas, and established
it upon the floods.
3. Who shall ascend into the hill of the LORD? or
who shall stand in his holy place?
4. He that hath clean hands, and a pure heart; who hath
not lifted up his soul unto vanity, nor sworn deceitfully.
5. He shall receive the blessing from the LORD, and
righteousness from the God of his salvation.
6. This is the generation of them that seek him, that seek
thy face, O Jacob. Selah.
7. Lift up your heads, O ye gates; and be ye lift up, ye
everlasting doors; and the King of glory shall come in.
8. Who is this King of glory? The LORD strong and mighty, the
LORD mighty in battle.
9. Lift up your heads, O ye gates; even lift them up,
ye everlasting doors;
and the King of glory shall come in.
10. Who is this King of glory? The LORD of hosts,
he is the King of glory.
Selah.

- Psalms 24:1-10 -

ACKNOWLEDGMENTS

Special thanks and appreciation to:

The grace of God that saved me and activated me for service.

The Holy Spirit, who has imparted to me the spirit of wisdom and understanding.

My lovely wife, Carol Holmes, for allowing me to use some of our time to complete this project.

Marion and Deloris Holmes, my wonderful parents, who taught me how to respect and appreciate all people regardless of the color of their skin.

Don Holmes, who again has been a source of help and for providing additional technical support.

Raymer Kelly, for being a sounding board and encouragement.

Christ Builders Church Family, for their prayerful support and encouragement.

My spiritual fathers and mothers, who instructed, nurtured, and counseled me during the formative years of my life.

Tivoli Community, for being an oasis of creativity and inspiration.

INTRODUCTION

Throughout the course of this investigative study, we will closely examine biblical passages, historical evidence, and weigh heavily the validity of other sources. My first encounter with the subject matter of this literary project was in the mid Eighties while I was serving active duty in the U.S. Army. It was further expanded upon during my six-year tenure with the Florida Department of Corrections. I was fortunate enough to have worked at two prisons which allowed me to witness a great deal of humanity.

After my transfer to the second correctional facility, the Holy Spirit began to impart unto me a very specific revelation concerning the diversity of mankind. I began to refer to it as the *Noah's Family revelation*. It was on a Saturday afternoon. I was assigned to Tower 3, overlooking the recreation field, when I heard softly the words, "Look at the nations!" I later understood that to mean descendants from Noah's three sons made up the prison population. The diversity among the inmates was quite obvious and could not be ignored.

The diverse populace of prisoners came with its own unique set of problems. Conflicts would arise as a result of the population's diversity.

Officially, at that time the Department of Corrections classified its thousands of offenders by race. There were inmates that were black, white, Mexican, Cuban, Puerto Rican, Jordanian, Palestinian, Dominican, Asian, and a host of Native Americans faring from various tribes.

An older viewpoint might report that among those incarcerated by the state were Negroids, Caucasoids, and Mongoloids. Later, in the book I will share my own experience with that particular classification and how it made a lasting impression on me.

I have learned that the human race consists of many different types of people, and sometimes those differences can cause contention, strife, injustices, and unspeakable acts toward your fellow man. None of the aforementioned things can destroy nor tarnish the beauty of *Noah's Family* which have become the nations of the world.

CHAPTER I
The Beginning

Thousands of years ago, there was a man born whose name was Lamech. He was the son of the oldest living human being recorded in biblical history. Yes, Methuselah lived to be 969 years old, then he died. Methuselah was the son of the renowned Hall of Faith inductee, Enoch.

Enoch was the man who walked with Elohim or God. His walk of faith caused him to be translated and not face death as others had done before and after him. Enoch was later joined in the Hall of Faith by his great-grandson, a righteous preacher named Noah. This was Lamech's son, who later grew to become a great man of God. He fulfilled an instrumental role in the annals of world history and the eternal plan of God.

Noah, a just man and perfect in his time, walked with Elohim, as did his great-grandfather. What a family! Men who could trace their lineage all the way back to Adam, the first man. This is the family from which Noah, the tenth person from Adam, descended. Noah was a builder, husband, and father. It is recorded in Genesis Report, 5:29 that Lamech called his son Noah because of the difficult times the old world (antediluvian era) was experiencing due to the effects of sin and unrighteousness. Noah's name, which means "rest," spoke of "comfort," for the whole world of his day was in need of divine relief and a comfort person. The LORD has chosen Noah to be the one providing comfort.

Enoch

The Genesis Report reveals that Cain's eldest son was also, called Enoch. He was Adam's grandson from a bloodline that had departed from the presence of the LORD. Cain built a city and called it Enoch after the name of his son. The City of Enoch is the first city mentioned in the Holy Scriptures. However, the Enoch who has impacted human civilization the most did not descend from the bloodline of Cain. Rather he descended from Seth's bloodline and is commonly known as the seventh from Adam.

This description is quite significant as it relates to the concept of divine completion and rest. Enoch, the Scribe portrays a type of perfected humanity that hungers and thirsts after righteousness. The working of God was indeed taking place in the life of Enoch. Enoch's name means, 'dedicated, disciplined' and can be pronounced Hanoch as well as, Henoch. According to the Apocryphal Book of Enoch. His life and ministry reflected extreme dedication unto the Most High God.

Holy devotion and discipline were witnessed in the life of Enoch by men and angels. The Book of Enoch gives an account of Enoch the Scribe interacting with men and angelic beings.

The ancient Book of Jasher portrays Enoch the Scribe as a great contributor to the Antediluvian Civilization on behalf of the King of glory. The Book of Jasher states that Enoch's soul was wrapped up in the instruction of the LORD, in knowledge and in understanding. It further stated that he would withdraw himself from the sons of men for long periods of time until the LORD spoke to him about coming out of his house and secrecy. The Spirit of God was upon Enoch enabling him to teach men the wisdom of God and his ways. Many came to hear his wisdom among them were kings of the sons of men, among them were the greatest to the least, princes and judges.

The same kings, princes, and judges asked Enoch to reign over them to which he consented. After, they all assembled there was one hundred and thirty that submitted themselves to his power and command. Enoch's saintly life brought about much peace among the inhabitants of earth. Book of Jasher, Chapter 3, section 12 states, that Enoch reigned as a king over the sons of men for two hundred- and forty-three-years wielding justice and righteousness while leading them in the ways of the LORD.

The ancient Book of Jubilees records the birth of Enoch during the fifth week, in the fourth year of the jubilee [522 A.M. or 622 A.M.], the Hebrew calendar begins with the creation of the world. AM, is an abbreviation for Anno Mundi, which is Latin for "the year of the world."

The Christian calendar commences with the birth of Christ with the abbreviation AD, which is Latin for "the year of our LORD." Jubilees further records that Enoch was the first among men that were born on the earth to learn writing, knowledge, and wisdom. He wrote down in a book the signs of heaven according to their months that others might know the seasons of the years and their separate months. It sounds as though he was publishing a type of Almanac.

Enoch was the first to write a detailed testimony. He testified to the sons of men that occupied the earth. Making a diligent study of the weeks as related to Jubilees, days, months, and years. He recounted Sabbaths of the years as it was made known to him. Enoch's testimony pertained to the future of humanity well past the impending Great Deluge. Enoch's entire life is epitomized in the Hall of Faith records. According to Hebrews 11:5 of the King James Version. It reads as the following: *"By faith Enoch was translated that he should not see death; and was not found, because God had translated him: for before his translation he had this testimony, that he pleased God.* Enoch's devotion and dedication to his King and Creator made him fit to not die the death of all mortals since Adam.

The same passage of scripture to include verse 6, in the Message Bible plainly says, *"By an act of faith, Enoch skipped death completely. They looked all over and couldn't find him because God had taken him. We know on the basis of reliable testimony that before he was taken 'he pleased God'. It's impossible to please God apart from faith. And why? Because anyone who wants to approach God must believe both that he exists and that he cares enough to respond to those who seek him."*

Enoch, the Scribe walked so close with God that perhaps the spirit of prophecy rested upon him causing him to prophesy an eschatological event. He prophesied to the population of that day saying, Behold, the Lord cometh with ten thousands of his saints for the sole purpose of executing divine judgment upon the ungodly. The Epistle of Jude, verses 14 and 15 provide a biblical record of the testimony that had been revealed to him.

Jewish Historian, Titus Flavius Josephus writes in his timeless classic, *The Antiquities of the Jews* that Enoch succeeded his father Jared having received the government [age] from him. Enoch later on delivered the government to his son, Methuselah, who in turn passed it onto Lamech. Josephus further writes that after Lamech had governed for several centuries he appointed Noah, the tenth man from Adam to be ruler of the people. Josephus inscribes the following words about the lives of antediluvian patriarchs, *"But let no one inquire into the deaths of these men; for they extended their lives along together with their children and grandchildren; but let him have regard to their births only."*

The SEAL Commission

It has been made abundantly clear in Genesis Report, Chapter 1, verses 26-28. That the first man and woman upon the earth were created in the image of their Creator but they were also, given a very special commission by Elohim. A commission is defined as *an instruction, command, or duty given to a person or group of people.* Their divine commission gave them dominion over all animals in the seas, the air, and all land animals even, the earth itself. The commission's parameters were very broad and extensive from the largest of animals right down to very small as well as, the microscopic ones. The language of the commission is expressed in verse 26; *"And God said, Let us make man in our image, after our likeness: and let them have dominion over the fish of the sea, and over the fowl of the air, and over the cattle, and over all the earth, and over every creeping thing that creepeth upon the earth."*

The word dominion is pronounced in the Hebrew language as *Radah* which means 1. to rule, have dominion, dominate, tread down even, to subjugate, and to cause to dominate. 2. to scrape out, to scrape, scrape out. This is why the LORD brought the animals to Adam in order to see what he would call them. The name that he gave to each animal became their official name. Adam as 'man' represents the entire human race as a whole. Therefore, all that Adam was created with and granted by the Most High was passed on to all future generations of humanity.

This includes myself, as the author and you along with many others as the readers. Genesis Report Chapter 1, verse 28 reads as follow: *"And God blessed them, and God said unto them, Be fruitful, and multiply, and replenish the earth, and subdue it: and have dominion over the fish of the sea, and over the fowl of the air, and over every living thing that moveth upon the earth."*

The LORD included a blessing in addition to giving man dominion over the works of his hands. The SEAL Commission grants us our dominion in the earth signifying that we had been crowned with some glory and honour as stated in Psalms 8:1-9.

Good versus Evil

The Genesis Report reveals that the LORD God planted a garden eastward in Eden. It was there he placed the man and soon to follow the woman. The garden of Eden was meant to be an extension or an annex of the Kingdom of heaven. A place that would reflect the beauty and glory of heaven on earth. Adam, the first man was created to be the crown of God's creation to be a manager of sort over the earth's resources starting at the garden. He was given dominion over the works of the LORD's hand. Adam represented in himself the whole of humanity that includes you, the reader and myself, as the author.

It was a garden filled with trees that were beautiful to the eyes and delicious for food. Among those magnificent trees were two, very special trees that differed in comparison. One, was the tree of life having within its fruit quite possibly the essence of eternal life and the other was the tree of the knowledge of good and evil. The latter tree did possess in its fruit the very opposite of life and godliness. We should note at this point that Adam and later on Eve, knew only God for they were clothed in light having no knowledge of good nor evil.

The knowledge of good and evil have always been the antithesis of the SEAL Commission causing mankind's dominion of the earth to be impeded and somewhat limited from reaching its full potential. After all, it was the consumption of fruit from a certain tree that the King of glory decreed would bring about death. It's too bad that Adam and Eve did not know the full measure of loss and death that would occur. Even, today as descendants of Adam and Eve the seeds from their consumption have been passed on to the entire human race. Looking back from the greatest day in human history which was the crucifixion of the Father's only begotten Son. We can see that death was connected to sin, darkness, absence of love and light. It includes a disruption of fellowship and communion with God making one's soul alienated from the life of God.

I am reminded of a television broadcast that took place on March 7, 1969. It was the original air date of an episode from the acclaimed television series Star Trek – The Original Series entitled; 'Savage Curtain.' It was written by Gene Roddenberry, Arthur Heinemann and directed by Herschel Daugherty. Based on the plot it was a most fitting episode, one that matched the turbulent times of the Sixties. The more powerful alien creatures conducted an experiment to determine as they viewed it. Which human philosophy was stronger: good or evil? Two opposing sides were formed for a contest to the death. The two sides consisted of historical figures from the past both fictional and nonfictional. The dream team of evil comprised of two fictional warlords, a practitioner of unethical experiments, and a true historical conqueror, Genghis Khan. The dream team representing good included three fictional characters and one actual historical figure, the 16th President of the United States of America, Abraham Lincoln. The host alien creature concludes that there was no difference between good and evil because the methods used to fight each other are the same.

The alien creature further remarked that evil retreats when forcibly confronted. It should be noted that this particular episode has been viewed as one of the series worst episode. However, as an astute historian I find the episode most fascinating and creatively insightful.

When we honestly evaluate human history do, we not accurately see what evil entails? Our military conflicts, murder, and injustice to our fellow man. Do not these things resound evil?

What about the legitimate effort to resolve conflicts with peaceful resolutions, respect for human life not as a political statement, and true justice for all? Is not the pursuit of life and peace more productive and fairer for a civilized society of humans sharing a planet together? Could it be that human beings are uncomfortable with the topic of good versus evil? These are very relevant questions and should not be limited to academia or a philosophical debate. This same contest has been consistently the drama waiting to unfold for centuries. It appears to be an inescapable reality for earth dwellers of any time period and place.

Thank goodness the King of glory has provided a reasonable solution for mankind one that is holy and acceptable unto him. We can find it directly addressing this ancient contest between good and evil in his Holy Writ. Paul's Letter to the Romans, Chapter 12, verses 17-21, he writes that Kingdom citizens should not return evil for evil. He urges that peaceful efforts should be the ultimate goal, vengeance should be avoided and left to the Almighty. Paul offers a very practical example when confronted with evil and an enemy. A similar method was applied during the life and ministry of Elisha, the Prophet. Finally, the apostle concludes the chapter with an admonition and an assurance that good will always conquer evil in the end.

Methuselah

As previously stated, Methuselah was the son of Enoch, the Scribe. The Genesis Report, Chapter 5, verse 21 records that Enoch was 65 years of age when Methuselah was born unto him. Diligent research reveals various meanings behind his name that speak prophetically about his life and things to come during his life span. Some of the meanings are the following:

- "man of the dart"
- "man of the javelin
- "death of sword"

A variant spelling of Methuselah's name is mentioned in the Gospel of Luke, Chapter 1, verse 37. It is spelled and pronounced from a Greek translation as Mathusala which means, "when he dies, there shall be an emission." Because the King of glory is the only one who can declare the end from the beginning. He is able to conceal a matter within the meaning of a person's name. This very same thing was done when he sent his only begotten Son to became an active participant in human history. Thus, fulfilling the divine meaning of Emanuel or Immanuel which is interpreted, "God with us."

It was through Jesus Christ of Nazareth that 'God was with us' in human history. He was with mankind in the likeness of sinful flesh during a crucial time in world history. Other biblical commentators add to the meaning of Methuselah's name as, "When he dies, judgment" or "When he is dead, it shall be sent." We note that 'it' is a reference to the deluge. The King of glory had concealed within Methuselah's name an indicator of when destruction would come upon a corrupt humanity and earth. My personal favorite is "man of the javelin."

Through that meaning I can see an image of the King of glory throwing a javelin or sharp projectile a certain distance in time. Once the javelin landed it acted as a precursor to an impending event. In this case the event was in fact the Great Deluge. The Most High made Methuselah's life span to be the javelin hurled through time in a powerful way landing on the shores of inevitability. It appears that Methuselah's prolonged life span was symbolic and evidence of God's longsuffering in the days of Noah.

The First Letter of Peter, Chapter 3, verse 20 speaks of the former, *"Which sometime were disobedient, when once the longsuffering of God waited in the days of Noah, while the ark was a preparing, wherein few, that is eight souls were saved by water."* Longsuffering is linked to the many divine attributes of the King of glory that essentially make him to be the sum total of love in the universe. It was this very thing that caused him during the time of Moses after Israel had committed a great transgression. To answer his petition so graciously by, placing him in a safe place in order that he might see his back parts (Read Exodus 33:17-23).

The longsuffering of God is mentioned again in the Second Letter of Peter, Chapter 3, verse 9 saying, *"The LORD is not slack concerning his promise, as some men count slackness; but is longsuffering to us-ward, not willing that any should perish, but that all should come to repentance.* The King of glory gave the Antediluvian Civilization plenty of time to repent and turn from their wickedness or face destruction. It is clear that after Methuselah died the flood waters of judgment came and brought to an end a very ancient civilization of mankind.

Lamech

The Genesis Report reveals that there were two men given the name Lamech. A name that means in the Hebrew language, "powerful, strong man, and for humiliation." Hidden within the Etymology of the name is an unused root meaning, "to be strong and robust." All of the aforementioned characteristics can be seen in both men. The first Lamech was born of the lineage of Cain, who is a murderer and the second Lamech was born from the lineage of Seth. The first Lamech took for himself two wives, who were called Adah and Zillah. This Lamech is the first recorded polygamist in the Holy Scriptures. He is the father of Jabal, the founder of tent dwellers and cattle owners.

His second son is Jubal, who was the father or originator of all that handle the harp and organ. Lamech's third son was Tubal-Cain, a very skilled worker in metals.

The evil and degenerate line of Cain was quite inventive and developed a seemingly advanced civilization apart from God. They had some culture and technology but like the original founder 'they went out from the presence of the LORD'. The second Lamech born from the line of Seth was rather the opposite in character from the first Lamech.

This Lamech was the son of Methuselah, and father of Noah. And the paternal grandfather of Shem, Ham, and Japheth, who are the progenitors of the human race until this day. He is later mentioned in the lineage of Jesus Christ as an ancestor. This is documented in the Gospel of Luke, Chapter 3, verse 36, *"Which was the son of Cainan, which was the son of Arphaxad, which was the son of Sem, which was the son Noe, which was the son of Lamech, (vv. 36).*

Lamech is mentioned in 1 Chronicles, Chapter 1, verses 1-3 among the antediluvian patriarchs, *"Adam, Sheth, Enosh, (vv. 1) Kenan, Mahalaleel, Jered, (vv. 2) Henoch, Methuselah, Lamech, (vv. 3).* Apparently, this history although very ancient was meant to be remembered by Israel for all of its existence. Now these same historical records are possessed by the Church and all seekers of truth. The words of the two Lamech's are starkly different in that the first Lamech spoke words citing vengeance, a matter that belonged solely in the hands of the Almighty. There is no faith nor hope in his speech only vitriol. It has been said that Lamech, the First was the world's first avenger.

He uses his power to speak to his wives about being avenged seventy and sevenfold. Thousands of years later the King of glory comes in the flesh as Yeshua Hamashiach and speaks something entirely different from Lamech, the First. The Messiah's words are verified in the Gospel of Matthew, Chapter 18, verse 22, *"Jesus saith unto him, I say not unto thee, until seven times: but, until, seventy times seven."*

They were words of instruction to the Apostle Peter, who asked a sincere and probing question about how many times must he forgive his brother of an offense.

Again in the Genesis Report, Chapter 5, verse 29. The words of Lamech, the Second are noted, *"And he called his name Noah, saying, This same shall comfort us concerning our work and toil of our hands, because of the ground which the LORD hath cursed."* Listen at the faith and hope coming forth from the mouth of Lamech, who was of the ninth generation from Adam through the line of Seth. Lamech's words are a rebuke to the vengeful and self-centered utterance that sounded forth from the first Lamech's mouth. The second Lamech saw in the birth of his son the possibility of some relief or rest from the unpleasant conditions upon the earth at that time. One Lamech practiced taking and the other one lived a life that ended in seven hundred and seventy-seven years (777).

Noah

As an historical figure Noah, the son of Lamech, father of Shem, Ham, and Japheth was alive during the Antediluvian Civilization. He was ten generations from Adam, the first man created by the King of glory. One biblical resource described Noah as "the new seminal head of mankind because his family were the only survivors of the flood."

His contribution to the history of man was pivotal because he was born prior to the Great Deluge but was influential to the emerging humanity that would assume the herculean task of Project Earth. The ground at the time of his birth was cursed and men were toiling by the work of their hands.

Now concerning the birth of Noah, a more than strange account is given in the Book of Enoch. Let us remember Enoch is the great grandfather of Noah and believed to be the author of the very ancient Book of Enoch which reveals extraordinary things pertaining to heaven and earth. According to the Book of Enoch, Chapter 106, sections 1-3, "After a time, I took a wife for Methuselah my son, and she bore a son and called his name Lamech. Righteousness was brought low until that day. And when (Lamech) had come of age, he took for himself a wife, and she conceived from him and bore a child. And when the child was born, his body was whiter than snow and redder than a rose, his hair was all white and like white wool and curly. Glorious <was his face>. When he opened his eyes, the house shone like the sun. And he stood up from the hands of the midwife, and he opened his mouth and praise the Lord <of eternity>." This account states that Noah's father was afraid of him because of his strange appearance. Lamech went to his father and begged him to go an enquire of Enoch, who was still alive at that time. At the time of Noah's birth Enoch was in isolation from men seeking the presence of God.

The Book of Enoch, Chapter 106, sections 12-14, "And Lamech my son was afraid and fled to me. He does not believe that (the child) is his son, but that (he is) from the angels of heaven. And, look, I have come to you, because from the angels you have the exact facts and the truth. Then I, Enoch, answered and said, The Lord will renew his commandment upon the earth, just as, child, I have seen and told you. That in the generation of Jared, my father, they transgressed the word of the Lord/the covenant of heaven, and look, they went on sinning and transgressing the custom. With women they were mingling, and with them they were sinning. They married some of them, and they went on begetting (children), not like spirits, but of flesh."

Enoch recants to his son, Methuselah that it was during the time of Jared that the Watcher (angels) descended upon Mount Hermon and crossed a line of no return. They were created beings given an angelic assignment that required their absolute obedience. They had forgotten that I AM is always watching and foreknew what they were intending to do. The account further reads, Book of Enoch, Chapter 106, sections 15-18, "And there will be great wrath upon the earth and a flood, and there will be great destruction for a year. And this child that was born to you will be left on the earth, and his three children will be saved with him, when all people on the earth die. And he will cleanse the earth from the corruption that is on it. And now tell Lamech, He is your child in truth, and <this child will be righteous and> blameless, <And Noah> call his name, for he will be your remnant, from whom you will find rest. He and his sons will be saved from the corruption of the earth and from all sins and from all iniquities that are consummated on the earth in his days.

This is the manner in which the Most High achieves things ensuring that a loyal remnant will always remain in the earth. This is the way of the Kingdom of heaven, *Thy Kingdom come. Thy will be done in earth, as it is in heaven.*

Bloodlines

The Genesis Report lays out very clearly the line of Cain unto the seventh generation but does not go any further. In chapter 5, the line of Seth is documented quite thoroughly unto the tenth and eleventh generation from Adam. Remember, Seth was the son that replaced Abel, whom Cain had slain. Two distinct bloodlines are featured in Genesis and ultimately throughout the Holy Scriptures. The vastly different bloodlines reflect that age old conflict of good versus evil.

It appears that the bloodline of Cain was advanced but wicked and corrupt bent on taking. However, the line of Seth was righteous and seemingly inherited a leadership role for the betterment of humanity.

Those descending from Cain's bloodline demonstrated a mindset that was contrary to the King of glory's will for mankind. While on the other hand Seth's bloodline demonstrated a faithfulness to their Creator's original intent and a willingness to submit to the King of glory's will.

Both bloodlines influenced the human populous of their day with two very different spirits. One blood line imparted to humanity a spirit of pride and rebellion. And the other, a spirit of humility and submission. Looking back in history, we can see evidence of such in the actions committed by descendants of Shem, Ham, and Japheth toward each other. Individuals and groups of individuals have acted as if they descended from Cain's blood line or Seth's blood line. Every facet of life and human society can be observed in this manner.

Those who choose in a given situation to act like Cain while others prefer the way of Seth. The New Testament Letter of Jude, Chapter 1, verse 11, speaks of the way of Cain centuries after Cain's death and the flood of Noah's day.

Jesus Christ was the King of glory in human form. He descended from Adam through Seth's blood line. He declared at the beginning of his inaugural address to potential Kingdom citizens things that were the total opposite of the way of Cain. Christ spoke of things like poor in spirit, those that mourn, and how the meek shall inherit the earth. The blood line of Seth displays a different attitude than those of Cain even, though they were brothers. And it should be pointed out that Cain was Seth's elder brother. Yet, in the Kingdom of Elohim the first shall be last and the last shall be first. It is truly, an upside kingdom!

Mesopotamia Method

It is defined by this author as a concept, viewpoint or perspective of viewing sacred and secular history together with the intention of developing a conclusion somewhere in the middle. It is believed that this type of balanced understanding can be achieved and that it is a fertile place for thought and reason. The Mesopotamia Method is a metaphor named after the infamous region regarded as the Cradle of Civilization. Located in modern day Iraq it was a portion of land situated between two legendary rivers, the Euphrates and Tigris.

Because of the close proximity of two rivers the soil was rich and yielded much life that led to invention, irrigation, crops, communities and great city-states. To view human history from only a secular perspective is just as incomplete as an eagle attempting flight with one wing. To see history from an entirely sacred position or understanding is also, inadequate for anyone seeking the truth. The Holy Scriptures reveal that the spirit of Cyrus, King of Persia was stirred into action by the King of glory on the behalf of his holy city, temple, and chosen people. Cyrus was an actual king who ruled a vast empire in the Mesopotamia region. Another instance, perhaps the greatest of all to demonstrate the flowing side by side of the sacred and secular.

It is none other than the life of Christ encountering a very real empire of Rome which has been described as a mixture of iron and clay.

Eventually, they collide at a literal crossroad in history at the place of the skull also, known as Golgotha. The King of glory was the first to initiate the Mesopotamia Method in order that sons of men might know that he is the Sovereign Lord, Yahweh.

Hard Times

My father, who was born in 1909 would often share with me what it was like for him growing up at that particular time. His recounting and those of his generation gave me an elementary sense of history.

They would often use the expression, 'hard times' thus, describing the difficulty and scarcity of those times. During Noah's generation, the earth was young and strong. Can you imagine the vigor and robustness that it must have had? However, mankind faced difficult times because the ground was cursed by the LORD and wickedness was rampant. Evil angelic forces had unrestrained access to the earth's realm. The Holy Scriptures state that every imagination and thought of man's heart was on evil continually. The demanding times that were upon the earth affected the entire human population. It was not an economic crisis, global warming or any natural or man-made catastrophe. There were no headlines of racial issues, pandemic, food shortages nor regional conflicts.

Adam's disobedience in the garden of Eden impacted every human being by passing on the legacy of a weak and fallen nature. Every human after Adam became joint heirs with him, equally sharing the consequences of sin and death. Through his disobedience, he unwittingly transferred the title deed of planet Earth over to the adversary, who is called satan or the devil. Death became the devil's soldier – his relentless killer for hire. Then sin became and still is the greatest "weapon of mass destruction" (WMD), the world has ever known. Thanks be to God, our Father, who sent his Son, Jesus Christ, to save the entire world from sin and death!

Because of sin, debauchery, and wickedness, Elohim began to prepare a Day of Judgment. There were probably no established courts or law enforcement as we know today. Without those particular elements in place to established law and order, that very ancient society became a very corrupt and decadent civilization. Yet Elohim, the King and Creator of the universe, was watching human history unfold. He was very much involved in the administration and oversight of his creation. Psalms 115:16 reveals a startling Kingdom reality, that the heavens are the LORD's *but the earth hath he given to the children of men."* Adam and Eve, the first couple of Creation, were expelled from the garden of God. The LORD placed an angelic sentinel, armed with a flaming sword, to prevent any reentry by mankind. He had already meted out judgment upon the serpent for his devilish involvement. Eve was judged for her participation in the offense, and finally, Adam received a stern judgment from the Almighty that is still in effect to this day.

Adam and Eve had in fact by way of choice committed the sin of rebellion and a treasonous act against the King of glory. They had followed satan's example of pride and rebellion against the very one, who created them. Later in the unfolding drama, death's first hit upon an unsuspecting mankind. It was exacted upon a lowly keeper of sheep by the name of Abel. (You know the rest of story.) Let us try and understand what this tragic incident meant for future generations of humanity. It was the very first homicide to take place on earth. Human blood had been spilled upon an already cursed ground. Cain under the influence of sin murdered his brother in a fit of rage. Abel, the shepherd had been slaughtered as easily as one of the sheep under his protection.

Like the act of treason and insurrection that was openly committed. It immediately drew the attention of the King of glory. Certainly, the senseless killing of the first human to offer an acceptable sacrifice before the LORD was a horrible deed. However, Abel's death spoke prophetically of what would occur several hundred years later involving the Son of God. Cain's dreadful act also, slew the potential descendants that would have been born through righteous Abel. Only the King of glory could hear the cries of souls yet, unborn from the blood spilled upon the ground. Immediately, without the assistance of an ace detective, a crime scene investigation unit (CSI) or a private sleuth.

Elohim, the King and Creator, who sits high and looks low, heard the victim's blood cry out to him. Once again, a divine court session convened with the Almighty presiding! A swift judgment was rendered unto Cain for his crime. His punishment made him a fugitive and a vagabond in the earth. The LORD set a mark upon Cain to preclude him from being killed for an offense worthy of death. Elohim's royal scepter was raised in judgment once again on Adam's family. The period from Cain's judgment until the time of Noah was a dark and chaotic time on the earth.

Because of mankind's sinful nature, the LORD decreed that his life span would be limited to 120 years of life. That decree was followed by the LORD changing his mind *(for it repenteth me that I have made them)* that he had made man on the earth. It grieved him to his great heart. By his own counsel, Elohim decided to destroy mankind, beasts, creeping things, and the fowls of the air, but Noah found grace in his eyes. Humanity as a whole continues to wrestle with the truth that the King of glory has the eternal right to judge his creation when he deems it necessary.

The King of Glory

This is one of the many holy appellations that are recorded in the Divine Library. The LORD as the King ascribes unto himself the majesty of possessing all legislative, executive, and judicial power manifested in its fullness as the self – Existing One. He is the heavenly Father, the source and foundation of all Creation. The LORD in his dealings with the fallen, anointed cherub (satan), Adam and Eve is justified by the right of creation. Right from the beginning it is the

LORD God who planted a garden eastward in Eden. The garden becomes an annex or replica of his throne in glory.

He demonstrates his full legislative power by giving Adam an absolute command saying, *'thou shalt not eat of it: for in the day that thou eatest thereof thou shalt surely die.'* As the King of glory, he issues a command that is binding upon Adam and Eve as well as, the future generations of mankind. His divine command delineates a boundary that is not to be violated. In addition to the command, he assigns a penalty of death without any possible reprieve or redress. In the Gospel of Luke Chapter 3, verse 38, Adam is identified as a son of God. No doubt it is for this reason that the LORD dealt with him as such. Therefore, as a son and member of the royal family obedience to his father was an utter requirement even, unto death. As the King of glory, supreme judicial power emanated from his throne. His judgment upon the serpent, the woman, and finally Adam was more than justified. Each one was the given an appropriate sentence that went into effect as the King spoke the very words of judgment.

The spirit of prophecy manifested in his sentence on the serpent signifying that *one* of Eve's descendants would be in conflict with the serpent's seed. The LORD's sovereignty and executive power is seen in his execution of the divine sentence on Adam and Eve for disobeying a holy command. The King of glory has at his command agents of enforcement which are a great host of angels. It is the King of glory who presides over the Divine Court and will not delay in intervening in human history. Especially, when the scales of justice are imbalanced.

You ask, "Who is this King of Glory?"
He is the LORD of Victory, armed and ready for battle,
The Mighty One, the invincible commander of heaven's hosts!
Yes, he is the King of Glory!
Pause in his presence
Psalms 24:10 (The Passion Translation)

The Fallen Ones

Before the creation of the first man and woman, a cosmic conflict was waged in the highest heavens resulting in the casting out of numerous fallen angelic beings. Their leader was Lucifer, who later became satan or the devil. The Hebrew prophet Isaiah spoke of many things pertaining to the origin of satan prior to his fall from the heavens. As stated earlier, Adam handed the title deed of planet Earth over to satan and the other powers of darkness. He (satan) immediately became the god of this world and the prince of darkness. He remained seated until the birth and death of Jesus Christ, who redeemed mankind from the power grip of the adversary of all men. Long before his fall into the darkness, he was created by God to be Lucifer, the son of the morning.

In the Hebrew, he was identified as *Halal*. This anointed cherub was responsible for praise and worship before the throne of God until iniquity was found in him, which led to his expulsion; however, he did not leave alone. A vast number of the angelic host rebelled along with Lucifer. The fallen ones were created in perfection and beauty. They abode in light and were at God's command but chose to rise up against the King of glory. Elohim cast these immortal and powerful beings into the darkness to await a far greater Day of Judgment.

Now, present – day citizens of the Kingdom of God can look backward from the cross of Christ to clearly see that those fallen ones are in fact the principalities and powers that Christ's Church wrestles with constantly in this present age. Satan and his fallen ones have been the dark forces behind the scenes influencing the affairs of men while lurking in the shadows of mankind's ignorance and fears. They are the forces that skulk about, seizing every opportunity to deploy their evil leader's ultimate soldier, Death. Jesus revealed that the enemy's sole purpose was to steal, kill, and destroy the LORD's creation. It was satan and his fallen ones that were the principalities, powers, rulers of darkness, and spiritual wickedness in high places during Noah's time.

His generation was ignorantly oblivious to the presence and involvement of such creatures. And their dubious effect on future generations of human society. They became the puppeteers wielding the jangling chords of deception. Succinctly, they were the proverbial "powers behind the throne." There was no one on the earth during that time who could unseat their devastating reign of terror, not even Noah.

The Days of Jared

Mahalaleel was born in the fifth generation from Adam and he was the father of Jared. Jared's name means, "descent or to descend" with root meanings of "to go down and decline." The King James Version of the Holy Bible provides a record of his life in the Book of Genesis and the Gospel of Luke. He is listed in the genealogy of Jesus Christ.

According to the ancient Book of Jubilees, Mahalaleel in the second week of the tenth jubilee took unto himself Dinah to be his wife and she gave birth to Jared. The Book of Jubilees Chapter 4, Section 15 (b) offers a chilling account of a significant planetary event. "… and he called his name Jared; for in his days the angels of the Lord descended on the earth, those who are named the Watchers, that they should instruct the children of men, and that they should do judgment and uprightness on the earth."

As stated by, the Book of Enoch Chapter 6, Section 6, "And they were, all of them, two hundred, who descended in the days of Jared onto the peak of Mount Hermon. And they called the mountain "Hermon" because they swore and bound one another with a curse on it." Enoch, the Royal Scribe describes an event in which two hundred angelic beings left their first estate and habitation to conspire against the one who created them. It was during that particular period of time that the human population increased drastically upon the earth. And the Watchers (Book of Enoch) or sons of God (Holy Bible) were mesmerized by the beauty of the daughters of men. They took human women as wives for themselves and beget children that became giants or *Nephilim* in the earth.

Genesis Report, Chapter 6, verses 1, 2, and 4 lays out its version, *"And it came to pass, when men began to multiply on the face of the earth, and daughters were born unto them, (vvs. 2) That the sons of God saw the daughters of men that they were fair; and they took them wives of all which they chose. (vvs. 3) And the LORD said, My Spirit shall not always strive with man, for that he also is flesh: Yet his days shall be an hundred and twenty years. (vvs. 4) There were giants in the earth in those days; and also after that, when the sons of God came in unto the daughters of men, the same became mighty men which were of old, men of renown."* In all, Jared lived a total of nine hundred and sixty-two years, second only to his grandson, Methuselah who live nine hundred and sixty-nine years. His lifespan was thirty-eight years short of one thousand years. Jared did not live to see the waters of judgment come upon the earth.

Grace

Although Noah was powerless against such a barrage from the forces of hell. The forces of hell barricaded themselves against humanity. Noah still found grace in the eyes of the LORD. His lifestyle and walk before God resulted in him being chosen for a special task.

The Bible records that the earth was corrupt before God and full of violence. Noah could not have at that time understood the full meaning of the grace of God. I believe he did understand that having divine favor really did make a difference amidst such hard times. Noah was born with a purpose, as it was proclaimed by his father at the moment of his birth.

Friend, that is exactly what happens whenever God's grace and your purpose connect. It will always equal the fulfillment of one's destiny. And destiny is what Noah was about to walk in! Right then, Elohim began to speak with Noah concerning his plans of destruction.

He instructed him to make an ark of gopher wood. The LORD was very detailed about the blueprint of the ark. He made it very clear about the type of materials that were to be used and the exact measurements. There were other specific instructions and details to be followed as well.

We can be sure that while Noah was building the ark, he was sharing with others the LORD's overall plan. A covenant was established with Noah, his family, and every living creature upon the earth. This was so because the LORD is covenant keeping God. Noah did according to all that Elohim commanded him to do and because of this he and his family were saved. It is written, *"Salvation belongeth unto the LORD: thy blessing is upon thy people. Selah."* (Psalms 3:8)

It was not the time for the fullness of grace and truth, for another was yet to come and intervene in human history. Nonetheless, Noah found grace in the LORD's sight and it was enough grace to save eight souls from impending judgment. It is written, *"For by grace are ye saved through faith; and that not of yourselves: it is the gift of God"* (Ephesians 2:8).

Forty Days and Forty Nights

And the LORD said unto Noah, *"Come thou and all thy house into the ark; for thee have I seen righteous before me in this generation"* (Genesis 7:1). There were provisions within the Noahic Covenant for the preservation of animal life. Animals designated by the LORD as clean were allowed by sevens, both male and female, to join Noah's family on board the ark. The animals that were not clean boarded the ark in groups of two – a male and female. The LORD further said, *"For yet seven days, and I will cause it to rain upon the earth forty days and forty nights; and every living substance that I have made will I destroy from off the face of the earth"* (Genesis 7:4). Please observe the King of glory's emphasis on the point 'that I have made'. In this passage of scripture, he expresses the right of creation as justification for his handling of humanity and all created life forms. This point of reality has been overlooked way too often by past, present, and future generations of mankind. The 'right of creation' clause is explicitly reserved by the King of glory as our Elohim, the

King and Creator of the universe, to intervene into human history as it pleases him. He does this for the express purpose of accomplishing his divine will. This I believe, is the great mystery about history that the LORD will intervene during any age of human civilization.

Psalms 29:10

"The LORD sitteth upon the flood; yea, the LORD sitteth King for ever." According to the Strong's Concordance the word, 'flood' used by the Psalmist David, Israel's shepherd-king is the Hebrew word *Mabbuwl: (*3999) [pronounced mab-bool'] means 1. Flood, deluge.

    a. Noah's flood that submerged the entire planet earth under water for about a year ++++ Some think Noah's flood was only local. However, the description of it found in Genesis 6 through 8 makes this patently absurd. If it was local, Noah had 120 years to migrate out of the area to safe ground! Why waste all that effort building a ship? With the possible exception of Psalms 29:10, this word always refers to Noah's flood.

What an awesome discovery revealed through the sacred language of the Most High God. Hidden within the Semitic language is a Hebrew word formed from certain letters of Aleph-Beit. Strong's states that this particular word is always used in reference to Noah's flood. The word is used (13) times translated as flood in the King James Version of the Holy Bible. Again, the King of glory is portrayed in Holy Writ as being enthroned or seated above the deluge that changed the world in Noah's day.

Psalms 103:19

"The LORD hath prepared his throne in the heavens; and his kingdom ruleth over all. Another psalm ascribed to David, son of Jesse, who is expressing that the LORD is a King that sitteth upon his throne

governing his kingdom. It is the Kingdom of heaven or government of God that rules over all human governments that occupy the earth. It is because of his absolute monarchy that gives him the right or justification to intervene in human history. The King of glory did intervene in Noah's day by sending a massive flood as judgment upon such a wicked and perverse generation. Centuries later the King of glory sends his Word in the likeness of sinful flesh. Jesus Christ was God, the Father intervening into the affairs of men. Modern historians will have to learn that the LORD can and will interrupt the flow of history when it goes contrary to his counsel. Humanity may not want to accept that there are certain absolutes when it pertains to the Kingdom of God. Still, their denial does not negate the reality that the King of glory can and will be an active participant in the history of men.

Therefore, in the six hundredth year of Noah's life, in the second month, the seventeenth day of the month, the fountains of the great deep broke, and the windows of heaven were opened. It rained upon the earth forty days and forty night.

Eight Is Enough

In the late Seventies, there was a refreshing sitcom featured on the ABC Network. The main character was based upon an actual person and his family. The fictitious family consisted of a father who worked as a columnist for a local paper. He was married and they had eight children. The series was called, 'Eight is Enough.'

Noah, the preacher and ark builder, was five hundred years old when his three sons were born. Like their father, they too had appointed dates with destiny. Shem, Ham, and Japheth were indeed Noah's boys all right! We have not discovered during our studies and research any evidence that might suggest that Noah fathered any other children after the great Deluge or Flood. We should point out the fact that Noah's three sons all had the same mother and were all married at the time of entering the ark. The Holy Scriptures (KJV) do not list the names of Noah's wife nor his daughters-in-law. This could be due to the reality of a patriarchal and male – dominated society. The ancient Book of Jasher 5:15 records that Noah chose Naamah the daughter of Enoch to be his wife. She was five hundred and eighty years old. Noah was four hundred and ninety-eight years old, when he took Naamah for a wife.

The Book of Jubilees states in the twenty-fifth jubilee Noah took to himself a wife and she soon bared him three sons. The Book of Jubilees also, gives an account in Jubilees 7:13-17 that Ham built for himself a city and called its name after the name of his wife Ne'elatama'uk. Japheth saw what his brother, Ham did and became envious of his brother, and he too built for himself a city. Japheth called the city after the name of his wife 'Adataneses. Shem remained with his father Noah, and he built a city close to his father on the mountain. The city was called after the name of his wife Sedeqetelebab. The three cities were located near a mountain each facing the mountain from a different direction. It is believed that the names of these cities are distorted for the reason of hiding the location of Noah's Ark. I urge each reader to consider all things before drawing a conclusion on what you have read.

Sound judgment based upon wisdom and understanding should be prayerfully applied.

Shem, Ham, and Japheth and their wives were all saved from Elohim's watery judgment, seeing that Noah found grace in his eyes. The following is written in the First Epistle of Peter, chapter 3, verse 20, *"Which sometimes were disobedient, when once the longsuffering of God waited in the days of Noah, while the ark was preparing, wherein few, that is, eight souls were saved by water."* We should pause and really ponder on the certainty that only eight souls were the sole survivors of the Antediluvian Civilization. One can be sure that it is the skeletal remains of humans and animals from that prehistoric time that many archaeologists have uncovered around the world.

The flood is a magnificent figure of water baptism followed by the joyful expectation of a new beginning. The wisdom of God speaks to us in volumes from a perspective and usage of numbers. Eight is a number that is filled with much revelation pertaining to the resurrection, salvation, and a new beginning, which is exactly what the Almighty wanted to do, and eight souls received it. Noah and his family were a new beginning of the human race upon the earth. Yes, Noah's family was saved by God from a judgment of water. Eight souls walking off the ark of safety was for certain a resurrection of humanity for the fulfillment of his original purpose. An old world of long - living titans had died.

A corrupt mankind perished in their sins and a watery grave. An earth that had been polluted was now washed and clean. Eight souls found refuge in a floating ark, while everything under the heavens was immersed into a baptism of water. The ark under Elohim's guidance and protection emerged on top of the mountains of Ararat, resting upon its peaks as if being resurrected from a tomb. Finally, Noah was the last of the titans or primordial ones who had been granted long life spans cutoff by, sin and death. At last, the first ones of the Antediluvian Civilization were washed away with the exception one 'titan' remaining. His name was Noah, the son of Lamech, grandson of Methuselah, and great grandson of Enoch.

Remember the Titans

NAME	YEARS OF LIFE	SCRIPTURE
Adam	930	Genesis 5:5
Seth	912	Genesis 5:8
Enos	905	Genesis 5:11
Cainan	910	Genesis 5:14
Mahaleel	895	Genesis 5:17
Jared	962	Genesis 5:20
Enoch (**Translated**)	365	Genesis 5:23
Methuselah	969	Genesis 5:27
Lamech	777	Genesis 5:31
Noah	950	Genesis 9:29

The same antediluvian patriarchs are mentioned in order followed by the three sons of Noah in the First Book of Chronicles. 1 Chronicles 1:1-4 bares record saying, *"Adam, Sheth (Seth), Enosh (Enos), Kenan (Cainan), Mahalaleel, Jered (Jared), Henoch (Enoch), Methuselah, Lamech, Noah, Shem, Ham, and Japheth."* Both lists are accurate and almost identical with the exception of a few names spelled differently but the same person. There are centuries between the account in Genesis Report, Chapter 5 and the version listed in First Chronicles, Chapter 1. This reveals the consistency of the Holy Scriptures as they were inspired by the Holy Ghost.

From the history of film there was an American biographical sports film produced in 2000 by Jerry Bruckheimer and directed by Boaz Yakin. It was based on the true story of the late, Coach Herman Boone and his attempt to integrate T.C. Williams High School football team in Alexandria, Virginia, in 1971. It should be noted that in America at that precise time the nation continued to grapple with the sickness of racism and its practice of segregation.

John Rolfe writes in a newspaper the following account;

*"at the end of August came a Dutch warship
that sold us twenty Znegroes"*.

American History Book

In the very state which was formerly a British Colony heralded as the sire of the American Republic. The famed Thomas Jefferson, Founding Father, principal author of the U.S. Constitution, and 3rd

President of the United States of America was a son of the colony of Virginia. What a sense of irony? History records that on August 20, 1619, the first enslaved Africans arrive in Jamestown believed to be from the Angola region of Africa. They were kidnaped by the Portuguese and are then bought by English colonists.

Approximately, three hundred and fifty-two years later an issue over race is still very much active having never been in remission. We, as members of the human race must learn that *racism is a sickness and a cancer in the body politic.* This truth was so eloquently declared to the masses by the renowned Preacher and Civil Rights Leader, Martin Luther King. *Racism cannot be defeated or eliminated without a pure understanding of the human race. Going back to the beginning in search of a sincere answer to this seemingly never-ending problem of race is a worthwhile endeavor.*

So, by reflecting on the Titans of T.C. Williams in 1971, we can direct the focus of our investigative study on the titans of the Antediluvian Civilization. They were primordial ones and progenitors of the human race. Noah is the tenth and final generation of the Antediluvians. After the flood the human race would be established through the sons of Noah forming three distinct branches of humanity.

Lamech's son had received a divine appointment and instruction to build a life – saving vessel. Unfortunately, it saved more animals than humans. He led seven souls and a great number of living creatures to their salvation from the wrath of the Almighty. Much in a similar way, Christ, the Savior – King, would do the same for all men upon the earth.

Noah, a preacher of righteousness, received a mandate from heaven for the good of the earth and its inhabitants. All good gifts come from above, that is from the Father of Lights (James 1:17).

What is a Mandate of Heaven? It is derived from the Chinese Civilization who is believed to have descended from the Sinite, who were children of Canaan. And Canaan was a son of Ham. The Mandate of Heaven (Tianming) literally meant, "Heaven's will" is a Chinese political and religious teaching that was used in ancient and imperial China to justify the rule of the King or Emperor of China. According to this belief, Heaven (Tian) embodies the natural order and the will of the just ruler of China, the "Son of Heaven" of the "Celestial Empire".

Apparently, the ancient Chinese people believed that the rule or government of a king or emperor could not occur nor be sustained without consent from on high. Noah had been given a divine assignment and a measure of rule to carry it out. Noah was made the governing authority on the earth after disembarking from the ark. He had received a Mandate of Heaven.

We should take note that perfect help and solutions for the daily lives of earth dwellers will always come from above. It is through the heaven and earth connection that our greatest hope is derived. One can truly understand the wisdom that the Apostle Paul was conveying to the church at Colosse saying, *"Set your affection on things above, not on things on the earth,"* (Colossians 3:2). It is Elohim who releases a resolution or Mandate of Heaven from the highest of heavens so that man by faith can bring about the results on the earth.

What started with Adam ended with one of his more prominent descendants. However, mankind would need another Adam to be born of a woman and sent to minister true relief and comfort to the masses, both born and unborn.

Heaven and Earth

> *"And so it is written, the first man Adam was made a living soul; the last Adam was made a quickening spirit,"* (1 Corinthians 15:45).

The world that existed before the great Flood needed an Anointed One. This fact remained true even after the flood. The human race continues to need a Messiah or Anointed One. The year 2012 and 2020 is no different than the days of Noah. The world desperately needs answers from above for its multiplicity of problems occupying our globe. That is why Christ declared in Matthew 6:10, *"Thy kingdom come. Thy will be done in earth, as it is in heaven."* Throughout the pre and post – deluge, not a man was born that could make such a saying. When Jesus came in the flesh he came with a Mandate of Heaven from his Father. Indeed, he was that true Son of Heaven that Chinese History spoke of. He could declare in John 3:13, *"And no man hath ascended up to heaven, but he that came down from heaven, even the Son of man which is in heaven."*

Yet in John 6:51, he would reveal more of his identity, *"I am the living bread which came down from heaven: if any man eat of this bread, he shall live forever: and the bread that I will give is my flesh, which I will give for the life of the world."* The generations that Elohim judged were starving deep within their mortal souls. They desperately needed a Savior and Redeemer. Glory be to God, our heavenly Father, who sent his only begotten Son for the salvation and deliverance of the whole world.

When the earth was new and potent, a time when mankind lived longer than three scores and ten (seventy years), the world that Noah knew had become sick and needed a supernatural healing. However, there was no Great Physician to be found. The inhabitants of earth were blind and impoverished in their spirits. They had great longevity but their souls were destitute. They needed the True Light! Noah's name prophesied of the comfort and hope that was lacking. He was a type of Christ for that generation, even a foreshadow of Jesus Christ. Jesus declares in John 5:37, *"And the Father himself, which hath sent me, hath borne witness of me. Ye have neither heard his voice at any time, nor seen his shape."*

The Beth–el Strategy

Genesis Report, Chapter 28, verses 1-22 gives a life account of Israel's third patriarch and founding father, Jacob. He was the son of Isaac and Rebecca, grandson of Abraham and Sarah. They were all descendants of Eber, who descended from Arphaxad, who descended from Shem. And Shem was a son of Noah. Jacob had obtained the blessing of Abraham from his blind father, Isaac. He was aided by his mother, Rebecca who loved him dearly. Jacob's brother, Esau was furious after discovering what his younger brother had done. This caused Jacob to flee from home with the patriarchal blessing intact. This blessing was highly valuable and was traditionally possessed by the next head of the family.

Throughout history acts of deception and treachery have always led to some type of conflict. Its for this reason that a different kind of strategy is required to bring about the peace between two or more disgruntled and hostile parties. The Beth-el Strategy is just such a stratagem. We can learn more about this policy and plan for intervention when an impasse has been reached. I believed for America and the world this problem of racism has brought humanity to an impasse. At this point we need to implement the Beth-el Strategy. The young patriarch, Jacob came upon a certain place during his sojourn from home. Think about it he would probably never see his father and mother again. We can be certain that stark reality was weighing heavily on his mind. He, no doubt contended with thoughts concerning his brother, Esau, who was now at odds with him over the right of inheritance. Jacob fell asleep and dreamed a dream that gave him a divine solution that would remain with him until the day of his death.

The place where he lodged over night was called Luz which meant it was a barren place with no sign of life. His conscious mind went offline in the midst of a dark and dismal situation. Nevertheless, Jacob's subconscious mind began to record the encounter with the King of glory whom he saw standing at the top of a ladder that reached from heaven to earth. Angelic beings were going up and down the ladder at the behest of their King and Creator. The words spoken to Jacob were similar to the words spoken to Abraham and Isaac reminding them of their appointed destinies and the Almighty's divine purpose for their blood line.

The King of glory's plan included Jacob inheriting a certain land, the multiplication of his descendants (seed), their coverage in the four directions of the earth, and how all the families of the earth would be blessed. Jacob was also given the assurance of the LORD's presence abiding with him until his words were fulfilled. After awaking from the dream, he had a different perspective about his apparent predicament. He had received from a dream a download of information and revelation from heaven.

That he could be apply to his earthly dilemma. His new insight inspired him to change the current geographical name of Luz to Beth-el which means the 'house of God'. Jacob declared it to the gate of heaven and he understood that he was not alone. His heart was filled with faith and a new found optimism. The Beth-el Strategy in regard to racism does require that humankind must first come to an impasse in their handling of this most dangerous societal illness. And accept the reality that alone they are incapable of dealing with this egregious dilemma.

The Beth-el Strategy will give America and the nations of the world a fresh perspective on race and how it has affected society as a whole. *This elevated strategy will point out how racism is counterproductive toward progress, economic growth, and just plain bad for the business of the world.*

My Three Sons

Again, we garner from American Film History the sub-title, *My Three Sons*. It was a sitcom that had a very successful run from 1960 to 1972. It was an ABC broadcast from 1960 to 1965, later it moved to CBS. *My Three Sons* featured the life of widower and aeronautical engineer Steven Douglass played by Fred MacMurray. During the series the character Steven Douglass was raising his three sons while working his career. This was my creative inspiration for the selection of a sub-title. It seems as though there is always three sons somewhere whether real or fictional. I know personally three brothers that also reflect the difference in personality and diversity of gifting as did Noah's three sons.

We will now elaborate on Noah's sons, their descendants, and individual destinies. I will not attempt to establish the natural birth order of Shem, Ham, and Japheth. To do so might lean more toward controversy and debate. Rather, the focus will be to show that each son was essential in the global effort of replenishing the earth. We will also unveil a pattern that demonstrates that God prefers to choose one or a few to save the many. Much of the historical data will exemplify that the order in which the LORD formed the first man, Adam (Genesis 2:7), is identical to the three brothers' and their descendants' trek throughout history.

The single abilities, talents, and gifts that resided in the generations before Noah were then endowments that were divinely disbursed and distributed equitably to Shem, Ham, and Japheth. Remember, all of their several abilities and gifts were embodied in the first man and woman. According to the account in Genesis, the LORD first formed the physical part of man from the dust of the earth.

This creative act of God correlates to Ham's strong beginning and his early descendants' dominance on the world scene. Starting with Nimrod, who was Cush's son and a grandson of Ham, they were the first to ascend in world power and domination. Their position of eminence was lost as a result of sin and disobedience. The Almighty does regard offenses to his glory and holiness as serious acts of defiance. In fact, they were considered guilty of treason against his Kingdom. This is a lesson that each brother's children would learn in history.

Secondly, the LORD breathed his own Spirit into the lifeless dust form of Adam. This action connects with Shem's descendants rising to a position of world supremacy and mastery. In doing so, they unseated Ham's posterity. The succeeding action in the formation of man appears to be a result of the union between lifeless dust and the breath of life from Elohim. Genesis 2:7(b) says, *"and man became a living soul."* The soul is the seat of our intellect, emotions, and will. This definitive act of creating the first man parallels the expansion of Japhetic nations and their ascendancy to dominance above the children of Shem and Ham. History bears proof that Shem's descendants have contributed to the spiritual welfare of human civilization. The sons of Ham have been steadily disposed to the physical well-being of humanity. Japheth's posterity has bestowed upon humankind marvelous mental and intellectual enrichment.

Our Kingdom Constitution or Holy Bible records so vividly very specific data of an ancient census, as it was revealed by the King of glory to his prophet, Moses. It is believed that Moses was the chief chronicler of all events written about in the Book of Genesis or what we shall refer to as the Genesis Report.

World History

The history of mankind upon this molten rock we call earth has been written from the period after Noah's flood until modern times by his descendants. It has been the offspring of Shem, Ham, and Japheth that have produced actions and achievements worthy to be chronicled. At times, the three brothers' descendants have been in harmony with each other and other times in disharmony. Many empires emerged from the hands of Semites, Hamites, and Japhetites only to crumble in those same hands. The kingdoms, empires, and fiefdoms of man are indeed fleeting with the passage of time.

The only Kingdom that is permanent and universal is the Kingdom of heaven which is ruled by the King of glory. It is his Kingdom that is the original Kingdom and government that all others are patterned after.

God's Kingdom is eternal and everlasting open to all that would enter in through their belief in Jesus Christ. Death, sickness, and war are absolutely defeated within his divine realm. *Righteousness, peace, and joy are the extended jurisdiction of the Kingdom of God through the Holy Ghost.*

True historians and chroniclers must come to understand as do poets and prophets that Elohim, the King of glory is an active participant in human history. And has purposely edited, revised, and rewritten the history of world. This he would do according to his counsel and pleasure. *History continues to repeat itself not so much because of human nature but because mankind refuses to acknowledge that the King of glory sits upon the throne of heaven watching over truth and justice.*

His majesty has commanded that the unseen realm will impact the seen realm (physical world). He has announced that darkness cannot prevail over the light for it must flee from its presence. In a world where history has been fueled by the hatred of one man toward another, one nation toward another nation. The King of glory has decreed that love will overcome hate in every setting and for all time!

An Ancient Census

According to the Table of Nations Population Authority (TNPA), there were seventy (70) nations that descended directly from Noah's three sons. Elohim used seventy (70) nations to repopulate and replenish the earth for occupation. The TNPA provides a registry of nations in Genesis 10:1-32. The Genesis account could be the first and original counting of the nations. It begins with Japheth and his sons and grandsons, followed by Ham, his children, and grandchildren. The registry is completed with Shem's family tree. Please observe below a manifest of the official Table of Nations Population Authority:

Japheth and Sons

[1] Gomer	[6] Meshech	[11] Elishah
[2] Magog	[7] Tiras	[12] Tarshish
[3] Madai	[8] Ashkenaz	[13] Kittim
[4] Javan	[9] Riphath	[14] Dodanim
[5] Tubal	[10] Torgamah	

Ham and Sons

[1] Cush	[11] Dedan	[21] Heth
[2] Mizraim	[12] Nimrod*	[22] Jebusites**
[3] Phut	[13] Ludim	[23] Amorite
[4] Canaan	[14] Anamim	[24] Girgasite
[5] Seba	[15] Lehabim	[25] Hivite
[6] Havilah	[16] Naphtuhim	[26] Arkite
[7] Sabtah	[17] Pathruism	[27] Sinite***
[8] Raamah	[18] Casluhim	[28] Arvadite
[9] Sabtechah	[19] Caphtorim	[29] Zemarite
[10] Sheba	[20] Sidon	[30] Hamthite

the first to establish a kingdom of man on earth
***the original founders of Jerusalem*
****oriental peoples*

Shem and Sons

[1] Elam	[11] Eber*	[21] Obal
[2] Asshur	[12] Peleg**	[22] Abimael
[3] Arphaxad	[13] Joktan***	[23] Sheba
[4] Lud	[14] Almodad	[24] Ophir
[5] Aram	[15] Sheleph	[25] Havilah
[6] Uz	[16] Hazarmaveth	[26] Jobab
[7] Hul	[17] Jerah	
[8] Gether	[18] Hadoram	
[9] Mash	[19] Uzal	
[10] Salah	[20] Diklah	

*father of the Hebrews
**the first son of Eber
***the second son of Eber also, an Arabian patriarch

Genesis 11:1-2, reports the succeeding information and revelation, *"And the whole earth was of one language and of one speech. And it came to pass, as they journeyed from the east, that they found a plain in the land of Shinar (see Daniel 1:2), and they dwelt there."*

CHAPTER 2
Shem: The Blessed One

Shem is Noah's son, whom we will refer to as *the Blessed One*! It was in the aftermath of a terrible human action of disrespect that set the stage of mortal history for centuries to come. It was an act that brought about the occasion for Noah, the patriarch to utter certain words that rang with destiny for many nations. Noah, the head of the family, had been dishonored by one of his own. The dreadful offense occurred while he was intoxicated with wine from his own vineyard.

This was a bit of folly on the part of the preacher man, according to Proverbs 20:1. We can't really be sure as to what state of mind Noah might have been in, having completed his primary mission of preaching and building an ark of gopher wood. Perhaps he was restless or feeling semi-retired from a long season of rigorous work. His negligence cost the family of man dearly. Hundreds of years later, a similar offense was committed by King David, who was a renowned son of Shem. David's sin incurred the judgment of God upon his household (2 Samuel 11;1, 2).

Noah's indiscretion has been just as costly for the entire human race. *A father should always strive to conduct himself in the proper manner before his children, especially his sons.* Different sources have offered their own perspective of what really happened that day in Noah's tent. For the purpose of understanding, we will present two such sources and the view given.

The first view identifies Ham as the guilty party, and the second view explains that Canaan, Ham's youngest son, wielded the act of contempt. Shem and his brother Japheth did the right thing concerning their father. The King James Version (KJV) of Genesis 9:23 gives this account, *"And Shem and Japheth took a garment, and laid it upon both their shoulders, and went backward, and covered the nakedness of their father, and their faces were backward, and they saw not their father's nakedness."* Talk about honoring your father and mother! Those boys did good and very good.

Many years later at Mount Sinai, another one of Shem's descendants received the Ten Commandments on behalf of Israel. These sovereign commandments included prohibiting the dishonoring of one's parents in any form or fashion. Yes, Moses was a son of Shem! This same son of Shem married a daughter of Ham, withstanding criticism from his brother and sister. According to our Kingdom Constitution in Numbers 12:1, Miriam and Aaron spoke against Moses's choice for marriage. Whether their reasons were due to the lack of covenant or the Ethiopian woman's skin color, the point is Miriam and Aaron were in opposition to Moses's union with the Ethiopian woman.

According to Genesis 9:26-27, Noah spoke with patriarchal authority, saying, *"And he said, blessed be the LORD God of Shem; and Canaan shall be his servant. God shall enlarge Japheth, and he shall dwell in the tents of Shem; and Canaan shall be his servant."* I believe Noah spoke from a position of headship over his family and the earth at that time. History bears witness that his prophetic declarations and decrees have continuously been fulfilled throughout time. The words uttered over Shem's life were indicative to the meaning of his name – a name that was given to him at birth. The Strong's Exhaustive Concordance pronounces his name (shame). From the beginning, in the English language, *Shem's* pronounced name does not sound very promising. Here is the complete Strong's explanation:

- Strong's number is 8035 or 8034;
- It is pronounced "shame;"
- Root meaning is "name" - - position; an appellation, honor, authority, or character;
- Also, meant infamous, fame, name, report, and renown.

The word "appellation" is a word not frequently used by most people. It is a noun meaning "a formal name or title" and stems from the

Latin language implying "to address." Elohim is more than awesome. He alone could have formulated such a plan that would put into motion such a purpose as having one son destined to have a great name or title above his two brothers. A second son would be destined to be great in the natural and physical realm, more so than the others. The third son would have a destiny of an enlarging or expanding action. Webster's Dictionary is one source that identifies Shem as the traditional ancestor of the Semitic people.

As you will discover later, each of the three brothers' names are very different. It is a well-documented fact that they were different. Their differences do not suggest deficiency, for they were equal in their strengths and weaknesses. Shem's name distinguishes him as having been granted something extra above his brothers. However, let us remember this distinction proceeds from the wisdom of God.

If Shem was given several portions above Ham and Japheth, it does not make him superior and them inferior. *It is exactly that type of unfounded reasoning that flows from the heart of racist thinking. Who is superior and who is inferior?"* It is all more baseless thinking to justify injustice toward each other. In a redemptive sense, Shem was given more than his brothers. Therefore, more would be required of him and his descendants in the grand scale of nations. Time warping ahead, many anointed men and women would rise from the loins of Shem. This would include the heavenly Father's only begotten Son, the Anointed One, Jesus, the Christ. According to the Gospel of Luke, Jesus is a son of Shem! This particular fact will be elaborated on more in another section of this book. The late, Dr. Arthur Custance, a Christian anthropologist, described Shem as "the worshiper." He is the spiritually enlightened one, chosen by the predetermined counsel of God to be a true blessing to the family of man.

Shem's Most Famous Son

Centuries later, Shem's greatest Son of all was born in a small town called Bethlehem. We have a witness from the Prophetic Record, Micah 5:2, records the following, *"But thou, Beth-lehem Ephratah, though thou be little among the thousands of Judah, yet out of thee shall he come forth unto me that is to be ruler in Israel; whose goings forth have been from of old, from everlasting."*

The Gospel of Matthew 2:5-6, declares, *"And they said unto him, In Beth-le-hem of Judea: for thus it is written by the prophet, And thou Beth-lehem, in the land of Juda, art not least among the princes of Juda: for out of thee shall come a governor, that shall rule my people Israel."*

This famous Son of Shem walked the dusty roads of Palestine, ministering healing and hope to the downtrodden. His actual place of origin was heaven, coming from the bosom of his Father. The Gospel of Matthew further records that he came down to mankind through forty-two generations, from Abraham to Joseph, the husband of Mary. He proclaimed the Good News of the Kingdom and performed many signs and wonders confirming the Word.

The Holy Spirit revealed to the Apostle John that Jesus Christ was manifested to destroy the works of the devil. His three-fold ministry of prophet, king, and high priest has restored what the devil had stolen from mankind. Christ as a bearer of three mighty offices is a direct reflection of the governmental functions of the King of glory. His ministry has victoriously resurrected that which the enemy has attempted to kill. Christ has successfully rebuilt all that satan, the destroyer, has torn down.

The Hebrew prophet Isaiah (Isaiah 9:6, 7) prophesied about Jesus's birth, purpose, and destiny. Isaiah did ascribe unto him various titles that foretold of his identity and more specifically about the works he would perform. Yes, indeed this Son of Shem preexisted before Shem and his father, Noah. Generations later, the Apostle John would reveal in John 1:14, *"And the Word was made flesh, and dwelt among us, (and we beheld his glory, the glory as of the only begotten of the Father,) full of grace and truth.*

Elohim's only begotten Son was born to fulfill the universal and eternal role of being the Father's True Prophet, King of kings, and our great High Priest. This same Jesus Christ was none other than the King of glory walking the earth as flesh and blood. As a Prophet, Christ could speak the absolute truth of the Almighty. Christ as King ruled and governed from a divine perspective. The Son, as our great High Priest, would be able to cover sin and touch mankind's moral uncleanness.

Truthfully, Jesus Christ, the Son of the True and Living God, is Shem's most famous descendant of all! I believe the meaning of Shem's name spoke prophetically of Christ's birth and his Second Advent. The Heavenly Father has given his Son, a name above all names – a name that will in the end require every tongue to confess and every knee to bow before him as LORD of all.

XXVI Nations

Exactly twenty-six nations (26) are recorded by the Table of Nations Population Authority (TNPA) as descending from Shem. They were the twenty-six that were designated by the Almighty to help repopulate the earth. It was twenty-six Semitic nations that contributed to the seventy nations designated by Elohim to get the human population thriving once again. The number seventy (70) has a special significance in the wisdom of God.

Seventy is a number that speaks of increase and addition. Wherever it is mentioned in the Holy Scriptures, abundance and multiplication are sure to follow. The Creator really knows how to initiate his plan and see it to fruition. If we apply a percentage to the number "26," we will discover that it is 37 percent of the number 70. This is most important, for it is consistent with the LORD's manner of using a little in order to save much.

Like a Creator – King, Elohim divinely appointed that twenty-six nations should descend from the bloodline of Shem. Let us be sure to ponder this fact deeply. *The LORD appointed twenty-six nations and not twenty-six races. Please keep that in mind.* As the Universal Sovereign, he has distributed to each of Noah's sons their own appropriate number of initial descendants as it pleased him. Each of the sons' individual proportions would help make up the seventy nations.

Afterwards, the LORD could use the seventy nations in order to repopulate and restock the earth with mankind. This deed was achieved through multiplication and divine increase. This act of God should remind us of the Parable of the Talents. Remember, it was the nobleman or lord that had arbitrarily decided what talents would be distributed and to whom they would be given. The root meaning of the English word *arbitrary* means, "judge, supreme ruler."

Elohim is the Almighty, the Creator of heaven and earth. He is the King of glory! The same is the Righteous Judge of the earth and the supreme Ruler of the Universe. Let the world's leading intelligentsia, its academia, the learned, unlearned, intellectual, and the most doubtful of this present age even, the fool. Know that Elohim has created all things for his good pleasure. We can be sure that Shem did not petition the LORD nor did he lobby for his father's favor, vainly hoping that Noah would use his influence to possibly sway the LORD's choosing. In the mind of God, it had already been decided before their births and before the flood as to how many descendants Shem's offspring would contribute to the seventy. We have learned from the Prophets that Elohim is able to declare the end from the beginning this is an attribute that distinguishes him from the 'lesser elohim' that he created for the purpose of serving him. One of the twenty-six nations descended from Eber, who was chosen for the advancement of the divine plan of redemption.

There were two sons (Peleg and Joktan) that descended from Eber. This same Eber was chosen by the LORD. These same men became nations, and these same nations became instruments of redemption in the hand of the Redeemer. This blessing was for the entire human race meaning, all of *'Noah's Family'*. It is also, known as the blessing of Abraham.

Now, let us reason for a moment from a scientific perspective that any type of replenishment and repopulation of the earth would require a new gene pool. The gene pool, by necessity, had to be large enough and possess enough depth in order to ensure a more diverse human population. I believe that Elohim, in all of his infinite wisdom and knowledge, had predetermined this factor to be included in the seventy nations. Infinitely, this act was done according to the predestinate counsel of the LORD, as written in Acts 20:27, 1 Corinthians 2:7, and Ephesians1:11.

The Tents of Shem

The governor of the earth, Noah prophetically stated: (1) Shem was blessed and Canaan was to be his servants; and (2) Japheth would enlarge and would eventually live in or occupy the dwelling places or territory of Shem. A tent is a mobile and movable temporary living quarters. A tent, since ancient times until today, has pretty much remained the same in purpose. Nomadic and migratory peoples have used the tent extensively. For thousands of years a tent has been the center of Bedouin life making it possible for them to survive the torrid conditions of the desert. The design has been somewhat modified even improved but its original intent and purpose is still the same. The God of the Hebrews chose to dwell or abide in the Tabernacle of Moses during Israel's wilderness years.

Sovereignly, speaking, Paul, the emissary, expounded upon the ultimate fulfillment of Noah's decree in the eleventh chapter of Romans. As you recall, from Shem is derived twenty-six sons. It was by a royal decree that the nation of Israel emerged from Eber. I am solely under the impression, that in all fairness and from an historical view. We should honestly consider what happened to the other twenty-five (25) or twenty-three (23) nations. We can be certain that some of the nations survived even unto this present day. Still others probably do not exist any longer, and some nations could have possibly merged into other nations both Hamitic and Japhetic in origin. Put a pin in the truth that other Semitic nations were born and do perhaps remain in existence until this day.

The Holy Bible, which is the Constitution of the Kingdom of God here on earth, records accurately the origins of those ancient nations and the eponyms that begat them. However, the Bible does reveal that many of those first-generation nations became bitter rivals and incessant enemies of Israel.

2012 A.D.

When we consider the early beginnings of American History and the collision that occurred between the native peoples, European settlers, and African slaves, could the Native Americans or Indians have been perhaps of Semitic origin? Research has determined that Ham's descendants settled primarily in Africa. In Psalms 105:23, the continent of Africa is depicted, *"Israel also came into Egypt; and Jacob sojourned in the land of Ham."* Japheth's descendants settled mainly in Europe and Shem's descendants mostly Asia. I am convinced that Elohim permitted America, from its colonial days until this present day, to be built and sustained by the posterity of Noah's three sons. Dr. Custance, in his *Doorway Papers,* suggests that wherever in the world that descendants of Shem, Ham, and Japheth work together in harmony, that civilization usually attains to its highest possibility of achievement, progress, and success. However, this entire supposition will require more attention and research.

Project Earth

The first family of the post-Flood era was given the awesome task of heading up the replenishing and repopulation of planet Earth. Eight souls had been selected to spearhead Project Earth. Noah and his family would be responsible for getting things going again. The LORD wanted them to *overspread* (Genesis 9:19 KJV) the uncovered landmasses from north to south and east to west. His command to them was, *"And you, be fruitful, and multiply; bring forth abundantly in the earth, and multiply therein"* (Genesis 9:7). It was to be a new beginning for humanity, one that was being orchestrated by the King of glory. It was to be the first global effort and initiative by earth dwellers. The Creator – King intended for eight souls to help resurrect the human population.

The earth that Adam was formed from, and because of him was cursed, had just received a baptism of water. Just imagine that the whole earth was then clean and ready for habitation. Continue to imagine in your mind how great the project was and how long it would take. The LORD knew very well that the primary mission of Project Earth would take hundreds and hundreds of years.

The Image of God

The Holy Bible indicates, according to Genesis 9:6, 7, that Noah functioned as governor of the earth and Chief Executive of Project Earth. He was responsible to the Almighty for the establishment of some law and order. Governor Noah was given the following instructions by the LORD, *"whoso sheddeth man's blood by man shall his blood be shed: for in the image of God made he man"* (Genesis 9:6).

Elohim reminds Noah that man was created in the image of God, which is exactly what he spoke concerning Adam. *"And God said, Let us make man in our image, after our likeness: and let them have dominion"* Genesis 1:26(a). Noah was expected to enforce penalty for the capital offense of murder. The Genesis Report in chapter 9, verses 28, 29 affirms that Noah lived 350 years after the flood. Another divine command had been issued to protect all men and the sanctity of human life. The command essentially protected the image of God that was inherent in all men since the beginning. Hebrews 1:1-3 speaks vividly of Shem's greatest Son as being the brightness of his Father's glory and the express image of his person, upholding all things by the word of his power. Jesus Christ is the truest reflection of the image of God. Because we are all created in the image of God therefore, in such a diverse humanity the many faces of Elohim can be seen.

The Tower of Babel

After some time, the prideful and rebellious ways of man began to resurface. It is quite possible that the bulk of the human populous had not spread out. It is widely believed that a grandson of Ham led the way in the building of a city and a tower whose top was to reach unto heaven.

Mankind's fallen and base nature being void of the new birth could only drift backward into the depravity of sin. Noah, the comfort person for the family of man prior to the Great Flood. He was the very same man born the tenth from Adam completing his assignment. His sons and their posterity would have to complete Project Earth thousands of years, nations, and generations later. We, the people of earth, are we not an extension of that same posterity? *Racism in any form or manifestation whether it be black supremacy or white supremacy is a blatant denial that we, the nations of the world are Noah's posterity.*

Could Project Earth still be under way? That would be an entirely different subject altogether. As I write and attempt to articulate this great odyssey, am I not participating in the long-term mission and scope of that ancient project? It is my sincere prayer and hope that this literary quest will make life among the nations better; thereby creating a better condition of living here on planet Earth.

Dr. Custance's *Doorway Papers* submits that Shem's descendants were not completely involved with the Tower of Babel incident. It was during the time of the city and tower's construction that *the spirit of religion and political shrewdness* started to stir among the children of men. There will be more said about this later, after we revisit the infamous tower initiated by Nimrod, a grandson of Ham.

Families, Tongues, and Lands

The Babel incident marked the release of confusion in the earth among the children of men. Genesis Report, 10:21 recognizes Shem as being the father of all the children of Eber. If you will remember, Eber was a progenitor of the Hebrew nation. Eber's name means "the region beyond," and he was also a grandson of Shem.

Genesis Report, 10:31-32 summarizes the family of Shem and briefly how the nations were divided in the earth after the Flood. It is amazing how a single stream of humanity was chosen to be a channel of blessing for the whole human race. *If racism is allowed to exist and flourish unchallenged within the human family it will run counter to the blessing intended for all nations.* Deuteronomy 32:8-9 clearly states that the Most High (God) divided to nations their individual inheritance, separating the sons of Adam. It was the LORD who set the bounds for his people, Israel. The nations of the world were given over to the 'lesser elohim' as principalities and powers. These 'lesser elohim' are the fallen angelic beings who followed their leader, satan into darkness. These things were sovereignly done by the King of glory. Because of the covenant, the LORD says, Israel is, "my people ("ammi')." Whenever Israel fell into disobedience and rebellion, the LORD would say they are "not my people (lo'-'ammi)."

Acts 17:26 emphatically declares that all nations (Ethnos) of the world were made from one blood and are designated to dwell on all the face of the earth. The LORD has in summation predetermined their times and the bounds of their habitation or existence. According to the Genesis Report, chapter 10, verses 1-32, twenty-six (26) nations came forth from the loins of Shem. Can you imagine the total number of families and tongues that proceeded from the original twenty-six (26)? And how many of them still occupy the earth today awaiting the return of Christ? These families all help make up Shem's family tree. Perhaps some of the family branches have been removed by way of death and extinction.

It is quite possible that certain of the families of Shem did merge with other Semitic family branches. Other families might have directly merged into different nations, both Hamitic or Japhetic. Each occurrence is more probable than not, for there is evidence today. This fact is proven throughout the world as apparent in the beautiful diversity of humanity.

I am confident that all of Shem's family descendants do possess the same gift blessing as the chief progenitor, Shem. The same gifting that Shem had would be present and detectable in all of the twenty-six (26) nations that originally sprung forth from his family line. Those same character traits and special gifts would genetically transfer to all of Shem's future posterity. Therefore, no matter where they might travel or migrate, Shem's descendants will undoubtedly make great "spiritual" contributions to any civilization or society.

Christian anthropologist Dr. Arthur Custance describes Shem as the worshiper. As a matter of supposition, the Native Americans could very well be a distant descendant family from Shem's original twenty-six (26); a family branch that simply migrated from Asia or some other continent.

The Indians of North America appear to possess a certain spirituality that is unique and tribal. Many North American tribes believed in a Great Spirit or a Creator that was responsible for Creation and their lives. The American Negro which for the most part originated from West Africa by way of the Atlantic Slave Trade. Their legacy of slavery and degradation in North America apparently produced in them for several generations a type of spirituality. The many years of slavery, segregation, and injustice have imparted to African-Americans cultural identity as a type of 'people of the Exodus'. Sharing a parallel experience with the ancient Hebrews who were enslaved by the Egyptians (Mizraim), who were sons of Ham.

Culture

After the Tower of Babel episode, Elohim dispersed Noah's family into different parts of the earth. Each family unit was different from another kindred family, which is not unlike many modern families of today. Diversity in many aspects was present among the families of Shem, for that was part of the Creator's design. *Tradition, ideas, values, and other components of culture began to arise.* Noah's family moved from dispersion to migration, during which time various types of tongues or languages, dialects, and colloquialisms emerged. *Even the earliest forms of slang may have developed as mankind had to learn to communicate with each other.*

Communication was necessary in order to bridge the disunity and misunderstanding gap successfully. After the LORD confounded the languages, thereby bringing to a halt the unity that humankind had galvanized, various or diverse natural tongues and languages began to arise among the families of Shem. *These tongues helped to create customs, norms, and other workings of culture.* The lands refer to the geographical locations, areas, and regions occupied by the families of Shem. *The makeup, layout, and topography contributed to the further development of certain distinctions of culture. Allow me to recall some of my earliest memories of Social Studies lessons which provided me with one of the most basic definitions of culture – it is simply a way of life.*

Using your mind, create a mental picture of how the earth might have been immediately following the Babel incident. Just envision how strong the sun shined ever, so bright. How clear the air was for breathing! The earth's elements were stronger and more intense than in modern times. Fetal adaptation was perhaps a more determining factor and reality.

"Shem was especially blessed black and beautiful,
Hham was blessed black like the raven,
And Yapheth was blessed white all over
Pirqe De Ribbi Eli'Ezer – pereq 24 (Rabbinical Quote)

Divine Intervention ~ Phase 1

The hour had struck on the clock of destiny following the Great Deluge. In other words, an appointed time had come in the ancient history of the antediluvians. There is no doubt of a supernatural connection between the King of glory and the flow of time. In the hand of the Almighty there is an affinity with infinity, when it pertains to time and seasons. It is widely known among modern theologians and all seeking ones that Elohim dwells in eternity but has created time as a module or unit for mankind to manage and utilize wisely. This concept of the Creator and time is truly a Kingdom concept. The ancient Hebrew prophet Isaiah declared this so powerfully in the fifty-seventh chapter and fifteenth verse of his prophetic book. A host of preachers and theologians have expounded upon the extreme difference in the *Chronos* time and *Kairos* time of God. Isaiah is prophesying to the nation of Israel that the Most High God dwells in eternity, having neither a beginning nor an ending.

The die was cast following Noah, the father of a new human civilization. He made such a prophetic and profound declaration over his sons and the distant futures of their posterity. As the author, I am part of that posterity as is each reader that will join me on this quest for a short time. This perpetuity would be best observed by closely observing the interaction of nations throughout history and judging both the good and evil actions perpetrated by nations toward other nations. After all, when we really get down to it, it is really the family of man in conflict – being dysfunctional, having a family, even a family feud.

It is within those intricate workings that the LORD's arrival on a scene of mankind's downward spiral toward destruction occurs. This means that his involvement was paramount if *Noah's family* might be helped through salvation. This is a great saying from a book of wisdom, Psalms 74:12. The writer offers the following testimony, *"For God is my King of old, working <u>salvation</u> in the midst of the earth."* To study human history without seeing that there were many, many times that salvation was an absolute must. The history of war is a classic illustration to this truth. Let us consider the first human conflict it was between two brothers that being Cain and Abel. Since then, there have been civil wars fought almost on every continent. Brother against brother shedding one another's blood over something senseless. Most of time its over a difference of opinions, power or quest for land. The LORD did intercede on the behalf of Cain and Abel long before there was any bloodshed. The LORD warned Cain that if he gave his best offering, he would be accepted as his brother's offering was recognized.

Elohim further counseled Cain that there was a dark force lurking at the entrance of his life. What was it that the King of glory was attempting to work in that instance? He was providing for Cain, a way out of a potentially bad scene. A detour or exit from a very dark path of no return. It was a measure of salvation from an encounter with death. Obviously, Cain did not listen and killed his brother anyway. What if humanity had been open to divine intervention prior to World War 1? Perhaps World War 2 could have been avoided? Humanity would be worse off without the intervening hand of the Almighty.

It was predetermined before the very foundations of the world. How awesome is the King of glory? He is our heavenly Father and the same who sent his only begotten Son to shed his own blood instead of ours. Could that be one of the great lessons of history that if we accept his blood, we won't have to shed the blood of our fellow man. *Sadly, racism is a vain and wicked philosophy that rejects the divine intervention of the Most High God. Racism says, to the King of glory, you don't have the right to interfere.* We will determine who is superior and who is inferior on our own. Long before the dawning of the first civilization of mankind upon the earth, certain matters had already been decided based on the sovereignty of God. Before the Almighty created the heavens and earth, his will and Word was securely settled in the third heaven. (see Psalms 119:89). Like a CEO, the heavenly Father had written certain dates and appointed times in his eternal planner.

This planner detailed significant events that were soon to come, yet with a desired end. He uses his eternal planner to conduct the business of his Kingdom. As the Creator of all things, he has a way of setting dates and events for his own purposes and good pleasure (Thank goodness!). He accomplishes such purposes through timely births and deaths of key individuals. These individuals became the instrumentation of his divine will. Even, today this is still true for the LORD knows the purpose and plan of every individual soul born on planet Earth. Whether they were saints or sinners, they fulfilled the sacred purposes of the Creator and King of the universe, which is the will of heaven. It is as the Son taught in his model prayer, *"Thy kingdom come. Thy will be done in earth, as it is in heaven"* (Matthew 6:10).

Truly, the sovereignty of God among the affairs of men should be an accepted fact. His sovereignty is just as real as the sovereignty of any constitutional state or nation whether it be ancient or modern times. He is the Righteous Judge of the earth and can therefore become involved in human affairs if he deems it necessary or if petitioned by those in need of his help. We should note that American History does record that during the struggle for Civil Rights, that African-Americans not only did they petition their government for redress. They through their peaceful protests, marching, singing and praying did in fact also, petition the King of glory for justice. I believe the social improvement and progress witnessed in America is evidence that the Righteous Judge of the earth does incline his ear to the oppressed. No doubt there is room for more upgrades in the Land of Liberty. This powerful function should be viewed as no different from a higher court reviewing a lower court's ruling on a particular case. The higher court has the sovereignty or jurisdiction to review a lower court ruling if they believed it to be appropriate. The King of glory possesses the jurisdiction over the flow of time which determines the outcome of human history.

God, the Father arrived and intervened in human history thanks to the birth of three persons who happened to be the sons of Shem. His pattern is consistently recorded throughout the Constitution of the Kingdom which is the Holy Bible. The first of Shem's progenies was Eber, who became the progenitor of the Hebrew nation.

According to the Genesis Report, chapter 10, verse 25, *"And unto Eber were two sons: the name of one was Peleg; for in his days was the earth divided; and his brother's name was Joktan."* It is most interesting that the earth is still divided to this very day in the year 2021. Knowing human nature, it is certain that division will extend far beyond this present year. It has been literally nine years since Noah's Family first publication in 2012. The Genesis Report further reveals that the name of Joktan means "he will be made little." He was also known as an Arabian patriarch. That smacks a little like the sound of the so-called Middle Eastern conflict, which appears to be a conflict early on between two sons of Shem, which extended to the sons of Ham.

Later on, in history, smaller residual conflicts among other descendants of Shem, Ham, and Japheth began to rise. These regional conflicts varying from continent to continent have filled the earth with much violence and have left in their wake poverty, disease, devastation, and more strife. Oh, Prince of Peace! We welcome your presence. Let the will of thy Father be done in the earth. As Kingdom citizens, we are instructed to pray for the peace of Jerusalem, which remains the center of the world's contention. It is ironic that Jerusalem, the city of peace and righteousness will be in the end a city for all nations of this world that will accept Jesus Christ, as the King of glory.

Historical Memo

There exist two well-known historical photos that have doubtless fixed their place in the archives of world history. Many history textbooks have within their pages the 1978 and 1999 pictorial images of an American president attempting to broker peace in the hotly contested Middle East.

The first photograph is one of U.S. President Jimmy Carter standing between Anwar Sadat of Egypt and Menachem Begin of Israel. It was an historic accord that brought hopes of peace to a war-torn region of our world. That is another poignant lesson that history teaches the diligent student. This world no matter how good or evil it is. It is our responsibility with divine help to make it a better and kinder world. Each human effort implemented for good is the ongoing work of Project Earth. *When we use our gifts and talents for the good of humanity, we strengthened the family of man.*

The second photograph is almost identical but in a different time and with a new cast of participants but the same family of man. During the last year of his presidency, President Bill Clinton is photographed with Israeli Prime Minister Ehud Barak *(who is named after a judge and military leader during the period of the Judges)* and Palestinian leader Yasser Arafat. President Clinton pushed hard for a resolution. However, the goal of peace was not attained, and tragically, tensions in the region only escalated.

Still, the fact remains that there are two different photographs that are evidence in living color – historical proof that *Noah's family* is a reality and its apparent dysfunction is similar to that of a smaller family unit. Prime ministers Begin and Barak, are they not sons of Shem? Whether they became sons of Shem naturally or by way of conversion is not germane to the overall topic. In this occasion they represent Israel and Israel descends from Shem. Anwar Sadat and Yasser Arafat, are they not the sons of Ham that have descended from Mizraim (Egypt) and Canaan (Philistine / Palestine), Genesis Report, chapter 10, verse 6? Both U.S. presidents are descended from Japheth, the expansionist son. Again, Dr. Arthur Custance explains how Japheth's descendants have extended or enlarged into a significant role on the world's stage. All of these events could not be mere coincidences.

Before moving onto the next phase. Let us just for a moment return back to the family tent of Noah. I submit to the reader and truth seeker that the forward movement of human history was set in motion by all of the events that took place. Because from those three brothers would emerge three distinct branches of humanity. Those three branches would lay the foundation for human civilization and its development for generations to come. The most desired end would be that their posterity would work together in peace and harmony.

Divine Intervention ~ Phase 2

Once again, the King of glory arrived on the scene and began to work his plan through a man by the name of Terah. The Genesis Report informs us that Terah's father was Nahor, who was about twenty-nine years of age when Terah was born. What a proud father Terah must have been? Terah lived seventy (70) years, then he begat Abram, Nahor (II), and their younger brother, Haran. Genesis Report, chapter 11, verses 27-28 reads, *"Now these are generations of Terah: Terah begat Abram, Nahor, and Haran; and Haran begat Lot. And Haran died before his father Terah in the land of his nativity, in Ur of the Chaldees."* The family was together in Mesopotamia, which means "the land between two rivers." Today, that part of the world is known as the Fertile Crescent. Soon, tragedy struck the family in the form of death. It was the loss of the youngest son, Haran.

The reader and truth seeker should ruminate considerably that another set of three brothers are called upon to help set the stage for the Creator's master plan. The Father's pattern throughout the Holy Scriptures is still intact. The number three is of great importance in the wisdom of God. Terah moves his family from the Ur of Chaldees into the land of Canaan. Afterwards, the death of Terah completes Phase II of the LORD's plan, as it is written in the Genesis Report, *"And the days of Terah were two hundred and five years: and Terah died in Haran (the land of Canaan)"* (Genesis 11:32).

Divine Intervention ~ Phase 3

The Genesis Report further records, *"Now the LORD had said unto Abram, get thee out of thy country, and from thy kindred, and from thy father's house, unto a land that I will shew thee"* (Genesis 12:1). It is most fascinating that whenever the LORD does something new, he always speaks a creative word that moves things into action.

The word of the LORD has creative and generative power that registers for beyond the comprehension of man. Secondly, the word of the LORD brings with it light and direction. Thirdly, the word of the LORD contains within its essence, revelation and illumination, which is divine communication. Listen carefully and closely to what the LORD really said to this chosen son of Shem called Abram. He spoke directly to where Abram was presently located. Also, he spoked concerning his familial relationships and ties to his father, Terah. He required of Abram to leave the familiar surroundings of his kindred and sojourn to a land that would be later revealed to him. The reader and truth seeker should really ask what actually transpired when the LORD called unto Abram.

The heavenly Father spoke to a man called Abram; whose name means "exalted father." This event was not just happenstance nor an occasion that took place among mere mortals. This occurrence was one of a myriad of things that Elohim commanded after the counsel of his own will. In another place, the Genesis Report declares, *"And I will make of thee a great nation, and I will bless thee, and make thy name great: and thou shalt be a blessing."* (Genesis 12:2). The LORD revealed to Abram his will for his life.

Let it be known that Abram became the original founding father of a great nation that is still great even to this day. When the LORD called Abram, the nation that would later come forth from his loins was not known at that time by the ancient world. The nation the LORD was referring to would later become the nation of Israel.

Another significant point that should be raised is that Abram would be blessed and have a great name (reference to Shem) that enabled him to be a blessing to others. The final point to be weighed is how the LORD would bless those who would bestow blessing upon Abram. The reference to being blessed and having a great name is a revelatory link connecting him to his ancient ancestor, Shem (Genesis 9:26). The King of glory has established a Prophetic Network for himself that has throughout history acted as his mouthpiece and illustrators of his written and spoken word. God's Prophetic Network (GPN) is most impressive serving as his media mechanism communicating his divine will to mankind. His skillful use of this network is truly mind-boggling and totally awesome.

Sarah, Hagar, and Keturah

What could the distinguished and pioneering patriarch, Abraham, possibly have in common with three women in a single lifetime? What bearing could these particular human relationships have on world history if any? How could this possibly be a part of Elohim's master plan?

These are just the kind of questions that one should be asking in order to determine the spiritual impact on secular world history. If Abraham was alive today and residing in the West, especially America, the power of the press would be brought to bear upon his personal life. Journalism through tabloids, periodicals, photos, and biographical documentaries would scandalize his name. One such documentary might read something like this: "Abraham, the Father of Many, this is the *E-Hollywood Story*." The introduction would be followed by a battery of narrated film footage, a background expose on each person involved, and hopefully an interview from a former employee of Abraham, founding father of Israel.

Again, referring to the *Doorway Papers* of Dr. Custance. He states that Abraham had three wives. The Genesis Report is the major source of this information. Sarah was the first and original wife, who in her old age gave birth to Abraham's heir. It was Isaac that would carry on the covenant with Elohim. Isaac's timely birth ensured another link in an unbroken line of succession dating all the way back to Adam, the first man. The LORD ensured that the chosen blood line remain intact and pure. After his father's death, he became the vision bearer of the Promised Land vision. Genesis Report, 11:29 clearly identifies Sarai, who late became Sarah, as the wife of Abraham.

Genesis 16:3 reveals that Hagar, a handmaid of Sarai, was given to the patriarch as a wife. This arrangement, although a customary practice, was from a divine perspective, an arrangement according to the flesh. Genesis 25:1 reveals that Keturah, after the death of Sarah, became Abraham's third wife. According to Hebrew tradition (presumably based upon genealogical records preserved in the Temple prior to their destruction by fire in AD 70), Keturah was descended in the line of Japheth. Such records were priceless to the Jewish people, particularly where Abraham was concerned. This subject matter may require additional study and inquiry in order to be written about at a later date. Whether it is fact or not, the wisdom of God speaks loudly! The number "three" has great meaning, including the Godhead, divine completeness, and a perfect testimony.

The Genesis Report concludes that Abraham, the patriarch considered by historians to be the father of three monotheistic religions. The three being Islam, Judaism, and Christianity. These three have impacted world history in many dramatic ways even, to this day. Abraham at one time or another had been the husband to Sarah ("princess"), Hagar ("flight"), and Keturah ("incense"). This is more commanding evidence that the Almighty is indeed behind the affairs of mankind no matter the extent of our many errors. He is not deterred by our apparent weak natures nor our endless deviations from his original blueprint for the nations. *The King of glory's master plan for the nations of this world is according to his counsel and perfect will.*

Perfection is just what the governments of the world have not been able to attain for the nations. No human monarch, despot, no legislative body, no court, nor tribunal or a government by the people have been able to secure a lasting peace and harmony among the nations. It is arrogant, prideful, and rebellious for human civilization at any time in history to think they can exclude the King of glory from their daily existence. He wisely orchestrates and oversees the turn of events and tempo in which they transpire. He has a way of interweaving his will into Creation (Romans 8:22-25). This truth can be clearly seen when we view his dealings with the nations of the world from both, a sacred and secular standpoint. I remind you again of the words by the psalmist in Psalms 74:12. We must try and remember that the business of salvation, nations, and rulers of nations is the business of the Most High.

He is the Creator-King (Elohim)! He rules over the heavens and earth but has delegated to man the responsibility of the earth. Mankind or humanity, even *Noah's family,* have been given stewardship of the earth. Matthew 10:29-31 and Luke 12:6-7 record Jesus revealing some deep things about the heavenly Father's interest in his Creation. Jesus Christ declared that his Father was very much aware of all things. A tiny sparrow falling to the ground was not beyond the watchful eye of the Creator. He further opened to his followers that they should not fear because they were of greater value than a sparrow. It was Elohim who allowed his chosen vessel (Abraham) to father children by three different women, who just happen to be descendants Shem, Ham, and possibly Japheth.

It was His Majesty's way of ensuring *"And in thee shall all families of the earth be blessed"* (Genesis 12:3b). It was the divine will of a holy eternal Father that the descendants of Shem, Ham, and Japheth be baptized into his Son, Jesus Christ.

Today, around the globe, the Body of Christ consists of *Noah's family* in all its beauty, diversity, and frailty! Jesus of Nazareth has successfully governed millions upon millions of followers through the Spirit of Truth, whom the world cannot receive. *History records that Noah's family are the actors, participants, makers, and writers of all human history.* We, the people of earth, or shall I say "the whole human race," we are the occupying family of the planet. We are a family that has true worshipers and real infidels, scholars and fools, murderers and healers, builders and destroyers. The estimated seven billion that live on this earth are a diverse array of individuals, all created in the image of the King of glory.

Roots

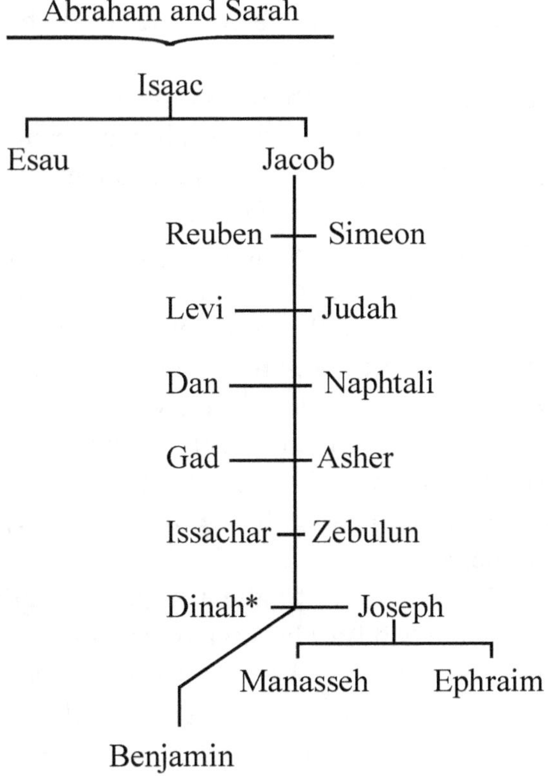

As claimed by the Genesis Report, it was the great-grandchildren of Abraham, the patriarch, that the LORD God used to form and birth Israel in the belly of Egypt (a son of Ham). The four centuries plus of Egyptian slavery and oppression served as a forge that melded together the descendants of the twelve tribes from a tribal confederation into a nation ready for destiny. It is simply another divine feat done by the hand of the Almighty.

I must point out that America with its colonial past and revolutionary glory did not emerge as a nation such as Israel. Although, I believe the American Declaration of Independence was a petition before the King of glory for the right to exist among the 'powers of the earth'. The signers might have had one perspective coupled with a little tunnel vision about the equality of man. Nevertheless, he granted to the representatives of the original thirteen colonies the right to exist as a separate nation. Elohim knew that what was to become the United States of America, a democratic republic would one day be a land of diverse nations.

Let's continue with the comparison of how the Almighty formed Israel beginning with a call to an exalted father who was the Godfather of the plain of Mamre. His name was Abram, who later became Abraham. He was given a promise and a blessing that he in turn passed on to his son and heir, Isaac. And Isaac along with the hand of his wife passed on the promise and blessing to his son, Jacob. For a season Jacob walked about with the same promise and blessing in addition to more revelation about the LORD's plan and purpose. There was a 'kindred factor' involved in the formation of Israel in a unique way they were all related in some way or another. A family of seventy or seventy-five migrated to Egypt because of Jacob's son, Joseph. He was sovereignly sent down to Egypt ahead of his father and brothers.

The Genesis Report validates that the entire fiasco was meant for evil by the hands of his own brothers but was rendered harmless by the King of glory. The great George Washington is regarded as the father of America and par excellent among the founding fathers. It appears that some American citizens may feel no 'kindred connection' to George Washington nor the other founding fathers. Unless they actually descended from them and are therefore related to them by blood. Moses, the great lawgiver and prophet was sent by the LORD to Pharaoh, King of Egypt. On the authority of Exodus 3:6, the LORD introduced himself to Moses as the Elohim of his father, the Elohim of Abraham, the Elohim of Isaac, and the Elohim of Jacob. In that instance on the Mountain of God, even to Horeb he connected Moses with the promise and blessing that he initially presented to Abram.

Moses was a descendant of the tribe of Levi. Miriam and Aaron, his brother and sister descended also, from Levi. Let us say for the sake of our understanding that the American charters of freedom convey to each person born within the borders of the United States a promise of citizenship and the blessings of liberty. Why have those citizens who are of a different nationality been denied their promise and blessings?

The question might be asked, Are the ideals of freedom, equality, and liberty enough to coalesce multiple nations to embrace a common destiny. Since the signing of the Declaration of Independence and other charters of freedom nations descending from Shem, Ham, and Japheth have journeyed to the United States of America. It will take the combine efforts of the three brothers' posterity to make America what it can be 'a shining city upon a hill'. How do we honestly describe the dark forces that push back against this worthwhile goal?

Elohim alone created the existence of Israel for there was no man that petitioned for their right to exist among the nations of the earth. The initiative began with the LORD himself so, he revealed to Abram that I am going to allow your seed to be a stranger in a land that is not theirs. During that extended time period they would serve the oppressor nation and be afflicted by them. He added that he would judge the oppressor nation and cause them to be compensated for their years of bondage.

Moses their deliverer led them out of Egypt after the fulfillment of ten plagues unto a mountain to receive Ten Commandments for them to live by. It was the King of glory that gave Israel their identity, culture, customs and sense of destiny as it related to the other nations. Did the Charters of Freedom give to America its identity, culture, customs and sense of destiny? It is a known fact that the founding fathers originated from Europe which is predominantly the land of Japheth, the philosopher. Israel was created in part to be a vehicle of blessing to the nations of world. Yes, the LORD created Israel for his glory and purposes which included the entire nation to be on mission toward other nations. They were to demonstrate the righteousness that the Torah was instructing them to shine forth to the rest of the world.

Israel was created to be a righteous nation totally set apart for the LORD. Genetically speaking ancient Israel consisted of Shem and Ham. Later the tents of Shem would be opened to sons of Japheth. *If America is to become a just democratic republic it must grapple with the evil of racism. Each American citizen must see that racism is opposite of the lofty values outlined in the charters of freedom. Racism stifles the breath of freedom and the responsible exercise thereof.*

America as a political entity may have been founded by descendants of Japheth but in order for it to reach the pinnacle of greatness it will require the descendants of Shem and Ham. I do believe the Almighty has ordained this point of truth and he will not change what he has decreed. At the roots of Israel's history, is Elohim. And at the roots of America's history, is Elohim. I conclude that because of those roots the posterity of Shem, Ham, and Japheth must be welcomed in both Israel and America.

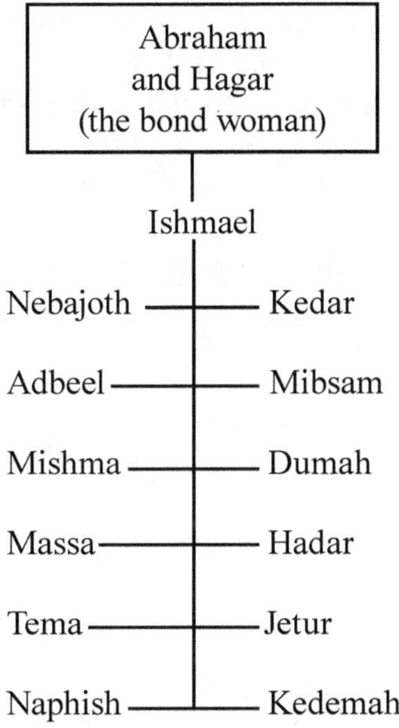

On the authority of the Genesis Report, chapter 16, verse 12 records this word of the LORD, referring to the destiny of Ishmael, *"And he will be a wild man; his hand will be against every man, and every man's hand against him and he shall dwell in the presence of all his brethren."* Like any concerned father for his children, Abraham talks with God about Isaac and Ishmael. *"And God said, Sarah thy wife shall bear thee a son indeed; and thou shalt call his name Isaac; and I will establish my covenant with him for an everlasting covenant, and with his seed after him"* (Genesis 17:19). *"And as for Ishmael, I have heard thee: behold, I have blessed him, and will make him fruitful, and multiply him exceedingly; twelve princes shall he beget, and I will make him a great nation. But my covenant will I establish with Isaac, which Sarah shall bear unto thee at this set time in the next year"* (Genesis 17:20-21)

This revelation about Ishmael's future, I believe, unveils certain things about the religion of Islam. From Joktan to Ishmael, from Ishmael to Esau, it appears the drama and action surrounding their lives point directly toward the never-ending tension between Muslims (Islam) and Jews (Israel). It seems that Islam is a rival religion and culture unable to coexist with Israel and Judaism. Could it be Isaac and Ishmael striving one against the other – one of covenant and promise and the other bondage and discontent?

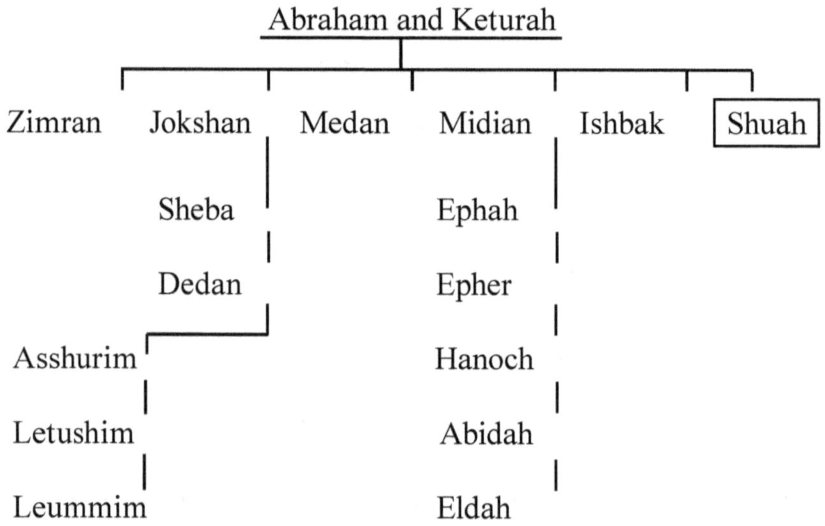

The Genesis Report gives an account of Abraham's final days, obituary, and those who attended his funeral. The days of Abraham's life were 175 years. His spirit was released having died at a good and ample age. His sons, Isaac and Ishmael, were present at his home-going. The *Kingdom Gazette* read something like this, *"And his sons Isaac and Ishmael buried him in the cave of Machpelah, in the field of Ephron the sons of Zohar the Hittite **(a son of Ham)** which is before Mamre; The field which Abraham purchased of the sons of Heth: **(a son of Ham)** there was Abraham buried, and Sarah his wife"* (Genesis 25:8-10). *"And it came to pass after the death of Abraham, that God bless his son Isaac; and Isaac dwelt by the well Lahai-roi"* (Genesis 25:11). Isaac and Ishmael cannot dwell together without the power of Jesus Christ. Nor can freedom and bondage exist together peacefully in a civilization, for one will cancel out the other. Liberty and tyranny are strangers within any civilized society boasting of the grand ideal that all men are created equal. Thanks be to God in Christ! Descendants of Isaac and Ishmael can become one in the *Ecclesia* of Christ.

Ike and Reba

Following the death of Abraham, Isaac is now the patriarch and head of the family. The headship and covenant responsibility were passed on to him. He was forty years old when he took Rebekah to be his wife. Isaac sought the LORD concerning his wife giving birth, and the LORD was entreated of him. Rebekah did conceive and the children struggled in her womb. This occurrence troubled her, causing her to become curious as to what was taking place. She enquired of the LORD in prayer and received her answer through a divine sonogram as only the King of glory can give. *"And the LORD said unto her, two nations are in thy womb, and two manner of people shall be separated from thy bowels; and the one people shall be stronger than the other people; and the elder shall serve the younger"* (Genesis 25:23).

The King of glory revealed to Rebekah the nature and destiny of the twins she was about to birth. Only the Creator can look inside a mother's womb and know what is to become of the offspring. Ponder carefully and deliberately, how the LORD identified the twins as progenitors of two different nations and not two different *races.* The twin boys, Esau and Jacob, were born of the same father and mother. Are they not both members of the one and only human race? So, how can we rationally and intelligently affirm them to be two different races? That would be utter nonsense and devilishly divisive. It has been that very thinking throughout history since the Tower of Babel that has helped to divide mankind from each other. Esau and Jacob are both descendants of Noah's blessed son, Shem. Remember, the twins wrestled in their mother's womb. Did not Sarah and Hagar strive against each other. Liberty and slavery, are they not opposites that struggle for dominance?

CHAPTER 3

Ham: The Physical One

Recently, I submitted a DNA test to discover some of my genetic and ancestral background. On the report of my profile, 88% of my DNA derived from West Africa, 11% from Europe, and 1% proceeding from Southeast Asia. The majority percentage from West Africa was the region of Nigeria. The Scotland region was the largest from Europe. The Southeast Asia region consisted of countries like Cambodia, Indonesia, Laos, Malaysia, Myanmar, and Thailand. Other countries from West Africa were Cameroon, Congo, Western Bantu Peoples, Benin, Togo, Mali, Ivory Coast, Ghana, Senegal, and the Southern Bantu Peoples. And from the European region they were England, Northwestern Europe, Wales, and Ireland.

This is an astonishing discovery outlining my personal story with regard to ethnicity. This specific DNA test provides evidence that I am connected to Ham because 88 % of my DNA originates from West Africa which is located in the land of Ham (Psalms 105:23, 27; Psalms 106:22). It proves also, that I am genetically connected to Japheth by 11 % with only 1% remaining. Could that small percentage connect me to Shem in some way? In addition to the previous findings, we have uncovered through diligent research that thousands upon thousands of Israelites from the Northern Kingdom arrived in West Africa by way of the Assyrian Captivity. Many tribal members say there has been an Israelite presence in West Africa since that time.

It has also been reported that thousands upon thousands of Jews from the Southern Kingdom migrated to West Africa around the time of the Temple's destruction in AD 70. The record further implies that the early beginnings of the Transatlantic Slave Trade was initiated by the Portuguese. Many believe that the first wave of Africans taken into slavery were descendants from the Black Jews who originated from the Iberian Peninsula. It has been stated that the Black Jews of Spain and Portugal were called Negro which meant black.

It appears quite possibly that the African American nation (ethnos) residing in America comprise genetically of Noah's three sons, Shem, Ham, and Japheth. In fact, this could be said about all the cultural nations and people groups of the earth. There may not be any that are pure Shem, pure Ham or just pure Japheth. This demonstrates the wisdom of a loving Creator making humanity extremely diverse and genetically connected in one way or another.

Just as the nation of the Israel was formed from twelve distinct tribes into a single nation until it was divided after the death of King Solomon. America, as a great republic is comprised of different cultural nations and people groups fused together by democratic ideals. The diversity among American citizens do not have to be a liability but rather an asset. By the hand of the King of glory, Israel became a united nation and by the same hand America can be fully united even with its diversity intact.

I have understood for a major part of my life the reality and significance of my African ancestry. If there was more to know as it relates to the Holy Scriptures, I was not privy to that information early in my rearing. I completed twelve years of my required education graduating from high school as a black student or Negro. I was not unfamiliar with other terms like colored or Afro American as well as, other extremely derogatory terms. I served a three-year tour in the Armed Services as a young black man proudly serving my country.

My family and community made sure that I was aware of the social inequities that stilled plagued America preventing it from being that 'shining city on a hill'. It was explained to me that it was your civic duty because this is your land as well as anyone else's.

Having certain insider information as it pertains to Ham and his descendants, we will make it very clear as to our intention. In accordance with the Genesis Report, chapter 6, verse 10, Noah is the father of Ham, and Ham is the brother of Shem and Japheth. Once more, Ham and his wife, *Ne'elatama'uk* were among eight souls that were spared from Elohim's watery judgment.

Ham had an active part in Project Earth right along with his brothers. It was Ham that is associated with the horrible offense done toward his father. No son or daughter should ever dishonor their parents in any form or fashion. To honor one's father and mother is the first commandment with promise.

To fully understand who Ham was and his part in the history of the world, we must begin with his name. A studious investigation of the meaning of Ham's name is a prerequisite for finding liberating truth. Like his brother Shem, the key is to understand what Ham says about himself and his God – given destiny.

Let us begin the investigation with a brief review. Shem's name means simply "name." That's right! Shem's name discloses that he will have position, honor, and a great name above his brothers. Likewise, Ham's name has the root meaning of "hot, warm." This meaning unveils to the student and reader that Ham would have a more physical orientation and gifting than Shem and Japheth. The Oxford Dictionary gives the meaning of the word *physical* as,

1. *Relating to the body as opposed to the mind.*
2. *Relating to things perceived through the senses (sight, smell, hearing, taste, and touch) as opposed to the mind.*
3. *Involving bodily contact or activity.*
4. *Relating to physics or the operation of natural forces.*

I am also certain that the meaning of Ham's name has a much broader application than rendered by Oxford. We should include in the name definition a reference from Egyptian antiquity, the words "chem, dark" for the duration of this section of study, particularly on Ham. I will draw from the Egyptian meaning of "chem" and conclude with the word *chemical*. As maintained by my research, chemistry had its early beginnings in Egypt or Mizraim. Ham's sons were Cush, Mizraim, Phut, and Canaan.

As we continue the investigation on Ham, I will use the words *chemical* and *blackness* as a means of expression and recognition. It is intended as a specific reference to Ham's physical gifting. We should remember that Ham's ability was given to him by the King of glory.

Elohim was fair and just in regard to Noah's sons, because the gifts and abilities given to them were really never about them. Rather, it was for the reestablishment and replenishment of the whole human race. All of this was done to the glory of God!

The Doorway Papers

Dr. Custance's *Doorway Papers* have ascribed to Shem, as being the worshiper, having great spiritual insights for the benefit of mankind. He accredits to Ham, the inventor (artificer, discover), that his posterity is the source of 3,500 of the world's known inventions. This evidence correlates with Ham's name and physical connotation.

In addition, it offers an explanation as to why Ham and his descendants have an innate ability to operate skillfully in the physical realm. Observe the wisdom of God in the meaning of Ham's name. It speaks of things physical and an understanding of natural forces. It would enable him to have inventive capabilities above that of Shem and Japheth. These same abilities would also be resident among his descendants to some degree, if realized and cultivated. Ham is the physical one, because his God – given name identifies him as such.

First, Elohim arbitrarily dispensed to him a special gifting for the good of human civilization. Secondly, the name given to him at birth reveals that his unique ability would be more adaptable to the physical realm. Thirdly, his ability points directly to the third part of man, which is the body. In closing, let us remember that man was created in the image of God. That very image is reflective of the Godhead – God the Father, God the Son, and God the Holy Spirit. The first man, Adam, was created as a tripartite being comprised of three parts. Each of those three parts correlates with Noah's three sons – the spirit of man (Shem), the living soul (Japheth), and the physical body (Ham), which was made from the dust of the earth.

A Personal Memoir

While growing up as a child in the South, I would observe the cultural differences between my black and white schoolmates. I can remember getting on the bus in front of my house. All of the occupants were black, including the bus driver. I can distinctly recall the treatment and responses from the other students. Through my observance, I noticed that black students tended to be more focused on the outward appearance. They would poke fun at other students' clothing, physiology, and their mothers. Most white students, on the other hand, did not display the same degree of tendencies. It seemed as if they would prefer to appear smarter than you instead of picking at your person. I should also add that children of all ethnicities can be cruel to one another for various reasons.

Later in my twenties, I was employed by a municipality, working with predominantly white employees. Many of them were from surrounding rural communities and quite familiar with the old segregated South. The equipment that we used would sometimes break down or malfunction. I do recall black and white co-workers using the term *nigger-rigging* or as others would say, *afro-engineering*. In the circle that I worked those terms were acceptable and deemed inoffensive. Although, the statements were very negative and had equally negative connotations indeed. However, the statements bear witness and do attest to the fact of Ham's descendants possessing an inventive ability, an ability that has enabled them to be technically more proficient. Ham is the son that the LORD gave an innate ability to work the physical realm. By creating and manufacturing useful devices, the living conditions of mankind could be improved.

Some years back, I was talking with a young black man, who was older than myself. I asked him if he knew or had heard of a man by the name of Ham. The young man quickly replied that ham (referring to meat) was too salty for him to eat. This account is more proof that many African Americans are ignorant of their true origin, cultural identity, and biblical roots. I am certain there would probably be a similar response as to the identity Shem and Japheth. Please take into consideration that there are still a great number of blacks who are still in the dark (no pun intended) about who they really are. Just imagine how many whites are also ignorant and remain in the dark about the validity of *Noah's family.*

Years later, now a generation young blacks and whites are familiar with the name of Ham, in at least two regards. First, there is an urban use of the name as a vulgar acronym (HAM). This has been popularized in some rap lyrics and has become a part of the pop culture vernacular. Secondly, Ham is connected to another urban or pop culture expression describing someone engaged in folly, frolic or just being silly.

Back to the Garden

Before we can continue our trek for truth, we must return to the garden of God, where mankind began. The Genesis Report records divine revelation as it was revealed to the great Hebrew spokesman, Moses who was a son of Shem. The Creation narrative is completely documented in the first chapter of the Book of Genesis. Day by day, a different aspect of Creation is spoken into existence by the King of glory. The Father, the Son, and the Holy Spirit were all present during the Creation process. Jesus was there, but he did not have a physical body. Nor was he known as Jesus but rather the Word. His appointed time to enter human history as a legal son of Adam had not come yet, although his entry and path was definitely on the horizon of civilization. It was hidden in the mind of Elohim, waiting to be manifested in the heavens and earth.

After the Great Flood, the heavenly Father was doing two things which are totally awesome! Like a major news network of today covering two events in different locations around the world. The King of glory was restarting human civilization on earth with all its inherent flaws, while simultaneously preparing a way for his Son to enter humanity. His entrance was for the sole purpose of working salvation in the midst of the earth thus saving the world from the ultimate destruction.

So, everything created was done so by the Word of Elohim *"and upholding all things by the word of his power."* And again, *"Through faith we understand that the worlds were framed by the word of God, so that things which are seen were not made of things which do appear"* (Hebrews 11:3). Finally, on the sixth day, mankind was born! Happy Birthday, Adam, son of God! To understand Ham's full capabilities, one must revisit the man called Adam. On the authority of Genesis Report, chapter 2, verse 7 it bears record, *"And the LORD God formed man of the dust of the ground, and breathed into his nostrils the breath of life; and man became a living soul."*

If we believe verse 7 to be entirely accurate, then observe very closely the order in which Adam's various parts are knitted together by the wisdom of the Almighty. Beginning first with his physical body, the Creator formed a physical body from the dust of the ground. Man's physical body is like a shell, a vessel or vehicle for the spirit and soul. *It has been said many times over that man is really a spirit housed in a body with a living soul.* I have found that profound truth to be very informative and liberating about the fulness of man's potential. Meticulously, speaking the human body from its very beginning is a lifeless shell.

Then the LORD took Adam's empty body that was void of life and locomotion. He breathed from his own Spirit of Life (*ruach*) into man's nostrils. All of a sudden, Adam inhaled and exhaled, followed by a pulse and vital signs. Yes, the first man was alive and well! It seemed as though the Almighty may have performed the first CPR on an unconscious person. The Genesis Report goes on to read that after the breath of Elohim entered the lifeless sculpture of the first man, his soul came online making him fully functional. For the sake of our investigation, let's review the following points carefully:

- Adam's body was formed from the dust of the ground. (Consider Ham, son of Noah.)

- Then Elohim breathed the breath of life into his lifeless form. (Consider Shem, son of Noah.)
- Then man became a living soul. (Consider Japheth, son of Noah.)

History offers a point of view that Adam's creative design flows parallel to Noah's three son's growth and development from antiquity to the present. Sacred and secular history side by side illustrate the rise and fall of each son's descendants as they carve out a path through time. Beginning at their father's tent, then onto the debacle at Babel, which caused the nations to be divided. The three brother's successive nations, kingdoms, and empires had their separate periods of world dominance. After close observation one will see that those periods of dominance do correlate with the creative order of Adam. We should note here that everything the King of glory has done in human history does reflect a divine order. As King of the Universe, the heavens and earth, his Kingdom is established in order and righteousness.

His divine order has within it a detailed pattern and patterns as to how he may accomplish his will. The amazing formation of Adam's body relates to the physical and technical capability of Ham. According to one source, the descendants of Ham founded fourteen (14) of the world's first civilizations. It was Nimrod, a grandson of Ham, who initiated the city and tower building program that later became the Tower of Babel. It appears that the sons of Ham were first but now have been viewed as last.

Nimrod: A Mighty Hunter

Nimrod's birth certificate, recorded in the Genesis Report, chapter 10, verses 8-10, identify Cush as his father. And Cush's father was Ham, who was a son of Noah. And Noah was the tenth man from Adam and the last of the long-living titans (antediluvians). Cush is the ancient name for none other than Ethiopia.

The Book of Genesis says that Nimrod began to be a mighty one in the earth. Just listen to the emphasis about who and what Nimrod had become long ago on those ancient plains of Shinar. Both sacred and secular history will recognize this son of Cush as a man of many names associated with myths, legends, and idolatry. This concludes a preliminary description of Nimrod based upon the King James Version as its principal source of information.

Supplementary sacred texts and writings will provide the truth seeker with a broader perspective of this phenomenal biblical and historical character.

Nimrod the Empire Builder

Thus far, we have described Nimrod in such striking terms as to grasp the student's attention while digging for more understanding as to his place in history. To begin with we have depicted him as one possessing the keen ability to work the physical and natural realm with great skill. This we should expect from a descendant of Ham. We can review thousands of years of African history especially, Kush and Ethiopia. And we would discover very powerful Warrior – Kings and Queens. This would prove to be so across the entire continent.

The Amplified Bible reads in the following manner: *(vv. 8) "Cush became the father of Nimrod; he was **first** to be a mighty man on the earth."* Please note that he was first, but keep in mind what the Son taught when he came in flesh. For instance, the first shall be last and the last shall be first. This is a great Kingdom principle established by the King of glory. There other equally powerful teachings by our Savior and King.

Jesus taught if you want to be great, then you must be a servant to others. Again, he taught that followers or citizens of his Kingdom must love their enemies and not hate them. *It is exactly the disobedience to the command of love that has fanned the flames of hatred among the nations of this world.* The human defiance of this most sacred command has help to ensure that Racism will remain alive and well within the global community. Racism of any sort is anti-Christ and anti-Kingdom. Christ also, taught that elevation and promotion in the Kingdom of God is a result of servitude and not altitude.

This entire *revelation of Noah's Family* must be fully understood from a Kingdom perspective. Even the course of this investigative study should be governed by principles and spiritual laws that are set within the Kingdom of God. Yes, the Kingdom of heaven which is synonymous with the Kingdom of God was in full existence during the days of Noah. The King of glory is eternal therefore, his Kingdom or government is eternal as well. For this reason, one can be certain that things pertaining to the sons of Noah are founded upon the Kingdom of Elohim. As a scribe, I humbly submit to his will and way as I proceed to carry out his will for my life.

The distribution of gifts, callings, habitations, and appointed times are entirely in the hands of the Almighty. As the divine Monarch and eternal Father, it has already been determined what Noah's sons would become and achieve in history. And how each of their posterity would impact the course of human events. It is mere foolishness and ignorance to argue with the sovereign will of the Most High. The Amplified Bible continues with: (vv. 9) *"He **(Nimrod)** was a mighty hunter before the LORD; therefore it is said, Like Nimrod, a mighty hunter before the LORD."* (vv. 10) *"The beginning of his **(Nimrod)** kingdom was Babel, Erech, Accad, and Calneh, in the land of Shinar **(in Babylonia)**."* Have you noticed the word "kingdom?" If we apply the Law of First Mention (LOFM) to Genesis 10:10 this is the first listing of the word according to the Strong's Concordance. This word that is pronounced in Hebrew as *mamlakah* it means *dominion, the estate (rule) or the country (realm): kingdom, king's reign, royal.* How about that? Nimrod was the first man after the Great Flood to set up an earthly kingdom! There is no doubt it was a *religious and political kingdom* based on earthly wisdom. Nevertheless, Nimrod, a son of Ham, was the first to do so after the judgment by destructive waters.

Nimrod was simply living up to his name and Hamitic gifting, which he inherited from his grandfather Ham – a gifting and capability that is expressed through the physical realm. He used great technical proficiency and the fruitfulness of invention to start the massive building project. Biblical resources state that Nimrod's name means "rebel, rebellion or the valiant."

Today's vernacular characterizes Nimrod as a person who is very rebellious or ostentatious. The Genesis Report designates him as a mighty one, a mighty man, even a mighty hunter in the earth. When placing the word "mighty" under the microscope, we discover it is pronounced in the Hebrew language as *gibbowr (ghib-bore')*. It is listed in the Strong's Concordance as No. 1368, which means: *1. strong, mighty man; 2. strong man, brave man, mighty man.* The word *tsayid (tsah'-yid)* is listed as Strong's No. 6718. It means: *1. hunting, game (hunting, game hunted); and 2. provision, food, food supply).* The two words "mighty" and "hunter" suggest the physical more than spiritual or mental. The student should know that such insight is no justification for stereotyping or any preconceived notions about the descendants of Noah's three sons. This investigation requires that we establish in our reasoning and understanding that every human being on earth is a vital part of Noah's family. Any capable hunter will confirm that hunting does require one to use his mind for strategy, cunning, and stealth. Mental acuteness, great skill, and knowledge of the terrain as well as the prey is necessary. There is nothing inherently philosophical about hunting of any sort, but it does require the participant to use his mind. It has been said that Nimrod was a hunter of men, which is quite possible and more likely in order to build an empire.

Surely, one could conclude that he was a mighty one in the earth who probably hunted men and animals: (vvs. 11, 12) *"Out of the land he (**Nimrod**) went forth into Assyria and built Nineveh, Reheboth-Ir, Calah, and Resen, which is between Nineveh and Calah; all these (suburbs combined to form) the great city."* From the beginning, a son of Ham is demonstrating his inventive ability. We should note that it was this very building and land development activity that led to the building of the Tower of Babel.

What's That in Your Skin?

Based upon the insight provided by the Genesis Report concerning Shem, Ham, and Japheth. They were all born of the same father and mother, receiving chromosomes and certain characteristics from their parents. I believe that each of them more than likely had different amounts of a chemical substance called *melanin.*

This peculiar chemical underneath a person's skin determines pigmentation, eye color, and some much-needed protection against the sun's ultraviolet rays. Through wisdom and understanding, we can know very well the patterns of our Creator-King. Shem, Ham, and Japheth had varying amounts of melanin in their skin. Ham no doubt possessed the greater amount of the chemical followed by Shem having a lesser amount than Ham but a greater amount than Japheth. Japheth had the least amount of this unique chemical within his skin. These early progenitors of mankind passed onto their descendants' genetic traits and characteristics. What these fathers possessed was inherited by future generations.

Melanin

A vast majority of the world's population has been given *melanin* for protection from the sun's dangerous ultraviolet rays. The minority segment of the human population possibly has less or no melanin at all. The word melanin is of Greek origin and means "black." Melanin is actually a black chemical-like substance found under the skin of some human beings. It has been discovered that this black substance contributes to the pigmentation or skin color of human beings. Truly, the Creator is absolutely amazing! It is no wonder that the Hebrew prophet Jeremiah would ask, *"Can the Ethiopian change his skin, or the leopard his spots?"* (Jeremiah 13:23a). The answer is, "Of course no, he cannot!" Why? Answer: Elohim, the Creator of all flesh, has created the Cushite or Ethiopian with dark or black skin. Remember, the Ethiopian is a son of Ham.

Only by way of a supernatural occurrence could such an event take place and that would only be to the glory of God. The great weeping Prophet Jeremiah quite possibly did not know that there was a black substance in the Ethiopian's skin that made it dark in color. It is also a possibility that the Ethiopian himself nor any of Ham's immediate offspring were aware of this magnific marvel of human physiology. Again, the Almighty is an awesome God. Listen to the psalmist's praise in Psalms 8:1 (a), 9, *"O LORD our Lord, how excellent is thy name in all the earth . . . O LORD our Lord, how excellent is thy name in all the earth!"* The Ethiopian's black skin is so to the glory of God. Even in the animal kingdom, the leopard's spotted coat is for the glory of God. This feline could not change its spots even if it wanted too. The leopard's protective coat was given by the Creator as a form of camouflage, and it is a key component for the leopard's survival.

I am certain that straightway after the Great Flood and the Tower of Babel episode, the earth was freshly cleansed, and its elements burst forth with strength in anticipation of new habitation. The earth's elements were potent enough to affect mankind's physical characteristics and to cause certain physiological changes for many generations to come. Researchers, scientists, and other enthusiasts refer to this process as *fetal adaptivity.* This concept refers to the outside elements over a period of time leaving a genetic imprint on future offspring. We will not devote any unnecessary time on this aspect of our investigation attempting to ascertain the particulars. However, we will amplify on what we call the *Genesis Perspective.*

First, eight souls were spared a watery judgment by the King of glory, who decided to interpose himself upon human history. Secondly, the same eight souls endured forty days and nights of continuous rain as well as flooding. Thirdly, the eight souls exited the ark atop Mount Ararat. Fourth, we acknowledge that Elohim used eight souls to restart humanity. The fifth point of consideration is that humanity increased from eight souls to seventy nations on to the untold millions and millions of human beings that have lived and died on planet Earth. The sixth and final point is that the earth was revived and renewed after the flood waters receded.

All of these magnificent and mighty workings were done under the auspice of a loving and all wise Creator-King. It should be no surprise that mankind having received his physical form from the earth, the common mother of us all. Because of this physical connection to the earth mankind could, from time to time, be affected by the earth's elemental forces, so much so, that future generations could undergo certain physiological changes if the conditions are ideal.

It is no wonder that several thousands of years later, a son of Ham or Shem, who happened to be a preacher and prophet. This same preacher shared a dream with his own countrymen and the whole world that his four little children would one day live in a nation (or republic) that would judge them by the content of their character and not the color of their skin. The Kingdom Constitution records a magnificent, divine lesson rendered through one of Israel's premier prophets and intercessors.

Historical book, 1 Samuel 16:7, *"But the LORD said unto Samuel, look not his countenance or on the height of his stature: because I have refused him: for the LORD seeth not as man seeth; for man looketh on the outward appearance, but the LORD looketh on the heart."* (All praises to the Most High!) This is a great Kingdom Principle that is worthy of all consideration and our sincere acknowledgment. The young preacher was indeed correct for we see that his powerful oration was based on sound biblical truth.

The lack of understanding of this kingdom concept among the posterity of Shem, Ham, and Japheth have caused undue devastation down through the centuries. *For one nation to see another nation as inferior or superior based on the outward appearance is an injustice toward your fellow man.* Injustice in one place or relationship is a threat to justice everywhere in any setting. Humans must learn to view one another based on the character within an individual and not make a blanket judgment on an entire nation because of one member of that particular people group.

This divine concept can only be found in the tents of Shem and not from the strength of Ham nor the philosophical ideals of Japheth. Yet, this spiritual concept does not belong exclusively to the descendants of Shem but rather to the entire family of man. Adherence to this royal concept will stabilize a civilization as it relates to diplomatic relations between the various nations that make up a specific population.

Genesis Perspective Conclusion

Now think of the possibility of how earlier generations of offspring carried in the womb have been touched by *fetal adaptability,* a cognitive process whereby the genetic codes of physical and emotional characteristics would be transferred from generation to generation. From ancient to modern times, mankind was designed to pass things down, which includes the author and readers of this literary work. It is very obvious that what has been called Mother Nature and Father Time must both obey Elohim, the Creator-King of the universe. The beauty of Creation demonstrates the power and creativity of Almighty God, who is a loving Father, fully omnipotent and omniscient.

The Fairness of God

Can anyone accuse the King of glory of being unfair and partial in matters pertaining to the governance of the world? His handling of divine affairs is according to his glory, righteousness, holiness, and the absoluteness of his Law. In his Letter to the Romans, the faithful Apostle Paul wrote by the inspiration of the Spirit. If it were not for God's Law being absolutely perfect, mankind would not be aware of sin's negative effect. The heavenly Father really does know what is best for his Creation. Left alone in his fallen and un-regenerated state, man cannot comprehend the weight of God's glory, holiness, and the purity of his Law. Only those human beings who have been born from above, thus signifying a new birth, can really grasp the wonder, splendor, and majesty of the Law of God. Being born of the Spirit enables mankind to discern the truth and know his acceptable will.

Sincere citizens of the Kingdom are enabled by the Paraclete or Holy Spirit to understand divine affairs, whether it involves the salvation of man or his sovereignty over Creation. He created the human race for his good pleasure, but the first Adam failed. Therefore, it was necessary for him to send another Adam, who was not from the earth but heaven. The King of glory had a plan of redemption for fallen man and an eternal judgment for satan, as well as his followers.

For this cause, he sent his only begotten Son to be a Redeemer and a Destroyer of the works of the devil. Who can declare that Elohim is unjust in any of his doings? Are not his ways past finding out? Job and his 'talk show' friends thought they had figured out the Almighty. They soon found out that the Creator of the universe cannot be placed or contained in their little wooden (humanity) boxes of reasoning. He is simply too vast and too majestic! Why would they try God like that? Yet from the whirlwind, he spoke to Job about very detailed things, shedding some light on the topic of discussion.

The LORD spoke his truth through the youngest of Job's 'talk show' guests, a young man called Elihu. The lad spoke directly to his elders that were talking plain nonsense. God's fairness and equity extends to his distribution of special gifts, talents, and distinct destinies. This type of divine dispensation reflects the superiority of the Kingdom of heaven over the kingdoms of this world.

Historical book, Acts, chapter 17, verses 24-26 reveals a sovereign truth: *"God that made the world and all things therein, seeing that he is LORD of heaven and earth, dwelleth not in temples made with hands; Neither is worshipped with men's hands, as though he needed any thing, seeing he giveth to all life, and breath, and all things; And hath made of **one blood all nations of men** for to dwell on all the face of the earth, and hath determined the times before appointed, and the bounds of their habitation."* This section of the Kingdom

Constitution clearly shows that God measures out and administers his will to all the nations of this world. Those very nations are the descendants of Shem, Ham, and Japheth, no matter what continent they may currently occupy. I believe that Ham was just as much a part of human history as was the legendary Carthaginian general, Hannibal. He was more than likely a descendant of Ham, who was from North Africa. And North Africa is located in the land of Ham. They are still members of *Noah's family.* In fact, you and I are among their sons and posterity. All praises to the Most High!

Thirty Nations

A complete report of the Table of Nations Population Authority (TNPA) holds as part of divine record that thirty (30) nations came from Noah's son Ham. His initial descendants made up about 43 percent of the original seventy (70) nations used by Elohim to resume civilization. We have learned from the wisdom of God that seventy (70) is the number of increase. There are many examples throughout the Holy Writ, such as ancient Israel's seventy elders anointed to help Moses bear the burden of leadership. The same seventy elders of Israel remained in existence and later became the infamous Sanhedrin Court during the days of Christ. Then, there was the seventy days which actually represented seventy years of Jewish captivity. Likewise, the number thirty (30) is a number that speaks of maturity and ministry which amounts to distinguished service.

Let us examine more closely the varied number of nations emerging from Shem, Ham, and Japheth. Anyone who has ever been a serious student of the Bible knows all too well that the LORD is always working from behind the scenes to bring mankind into a place of complete deliverance from all hang-ups and holdups. The heavenly Father really desires to see his will be manifested in the earth. Jesus came in the flesh and taught, saying, *"Thy kingdom come, thy will be done in earth, as it is in heaven"* (Matthew 6:10).

When I muse on the significance of the numbers 26, 30, and 14, they remind me of some type of physical or chemical equation or perhaps a patented growth formula created to enhance growth in plants. The three numbers simply reflect the awesome wisdom and knowledge of the King of glory, which is past our finding out. Ham's thirty (30) nations appear to have formed the basis for a new gene pool and possibly the dispensing of melanin to future generations of humanity. It is strongly believed that Ham had more melanin in his skin than his brothers. It is for certain that the region Ham's descendants predominately inhabited was closer in proximity to the equator. Essentially being near the equator meant a much hotter climate; one that would require more melanin for protection against the sun's ultraviolet rays. Those nations that settled further away from the equator or in cooler climates did not necessitate additional melanin in their skin.

Shem's twenty-six (26) nations are very fitting for the worshiper. Japheth's fourteen (14) nations demonstrate how the King of glory can take the least of nations and cause it to expand far beyond his brothers' descendants.

The Service of Ham

Genesis Report, chapter 8, verses 15-17: Elohim commands Noah and his family to go forth from the ark. This command given by the LORD was the official commencement of Project Earth, which included replenishing the earth and rebuilding a new human civilization. Each of the brothers' special gifts and callings would be needed to fulfill such a monumental task.

The children of Shem initially served mankind by sharing great spiritual insights that could enlighten many civilizations. The sons of Japheth would later in impart on a mass scale to the entire world great philosophical thought and views. Nonetheless, the service that Ham would render to humanity and civilization was one of creative inventions and just as valuable. Ham's capability would allow his descendants to operate in the physical realm with great ease. Technical proficiency would be his forte.

World History affirms that it was Hamitic civilizations that were among the earliest civilizations and empires – dating from Nimrod's kingdom to the Roman (sons of Japheth) defeat of Hannibal (son of Ham) at Carthage. Whenever we examine history for evidence regarding the descendants of Ham, let us not be narrow-minded, assuming that all of his posterity would be of one particular complexion or skin color. This point will be elaborated upon under another heading. Much in the same way, Shemites, Hamites, and Japhetites should seek to work in cooperation with their heavenly Father in the same manner that Jesus Christ did. Such an effort would be one of the most climatic events leading up to the return of the King of glory during the Second Advent. Ham's distinguished service should be directed toward that very end.

The Curse of Ham

This is perhaps among the top ten mysteries within the Holy Bible. It is a mystery that has left many students and truth seekers bewildered, puzzled, and perplexed. To some, it is an open-and-shut case with no reason for continued discussion. Some regard it as a cold case having no need to reopen or continue to investigate because there is simply no conclusive evidence for a trial by jury. Still others honestly would like to know the truth behind the prophetic declaration made by Noah toward his son Ham. Many just choose to be silent and neutral on the subject altogether. Nations that have been motivated by hatred and a desire to assert their own cultural superiority over others have contended that their ethnicity was superior to another's ethnicity. These nations have very craftily and cleverly used the curse of Ham to justify certain courses of action.

This deceptive effort has been propagated greatly in Western Civilization through the intoxicating effect of the spirit of Religion and Politics. In a sense, the curse of Ham was taught from a Theological standpoint from pulpits and later became policy imposed by the state in the forms of laws, slavery, segregation, and apartheid. Slave traders embraced the doctrine that was developed by theologians that the African was an accursed race, believing it was their Christian duty to evangelize and dole out divine destiny on the black savages of the Dark Continent. It has been suggested that the African did not have a soul and was more like an animal. All of this no doubt made him inferior to the lighter skinned races especially, the white man. Many of the enlightenment thinkers during the European Renaissance held to these beliefs and sought to prove it scientifically by studying the various sizes of human craniums. These baseless developments led to many European explorations and incursions into the interior of Africa bolstered by this horrendous religious and political doctrine.

This apparent doctrine of devils helped to fuel an African diaspora, which may have included black Shemites from the line of Judah. There were also divine judgments meted by the hand of Elohim on other sons of Ham. These divine judgments are recorded in many of the prophetic books. Each judgment warrants a serious examination by an earnest student and truth seeker. It would be most appropriate to note at this time that the descendants of Noah's sons all experienced the chastisements of the LORD because of pride and rebellion. We must always remember that divine providence amongst the nations is in the hand of the King of glory, who is the sovereign Lord of the earth.

Now regarding the actual curse, it was really placed upon Canaan, Ham's younger son, which was Noah's grandson. We must refrain from needless speculation; we will attempt to briefly delineate the specifics of what really happened. Several events led up to the terrible offense directed toward Noah, who was the head of the family and the LORD's administrator of Project Earth. The Genesis Report states that Noah planted a vineyard and he drank of the wine until he was drunk. Drawing from two schools of thought, Noah himself was lying naked in a drunken stupor, or secondly, Noah and his wife were both naked in the tent. They were either discovered or mocked by Ham or possibly Canaan. Noah, the father of Shem, Ham, and Japheth was dishonored by one of his sons or a grandson. Imagine, here is a man well over six hundred (600) years of age being dishonored by one of his children. The spiritual law of honor had been broken, and the principle is that all sin must be atoned for. Much curious speculation has emerged from this passage of scripture to include homosexuality, incest, and castration.

It has been expounded upon the fact that Noah could not curse Ham without pronouncing a curse upon himself. Dr. Custance has presented very eloquently that this concept is very much embedded in Hebrew thought and wisdom. The relationship between a father and son was considered quite unique and special. The Gospels echoed loudly the close and deeply personal relationship between the heavenly Father and his son, Jesus, the Christ. Noah was obviously aware of the spiritual principle and did acknowledge it in this instance. So, the curse which came by way of a prophetic declaration was levied upon the youngest grandson, Canaan. Interestingly enough, Canaan's descendants were known for their heathen and sensual ways that were an abomination to the LORD.

There has not been a curse placed upon or directed toward mankind that the last Adam's death could not nullify. His death is the greatest single act of love in the history of the world. Jesus Christ is the last Adam and the Kinsman-Redeemer for Noah's family. He alone does what no other man has been able to do and that is set the human family back on course toward harmony and progress.

Ham Throughout the Bible

Let us make use of a long-distance glance at the Holy Scriptures based upon the King James Version (KJV), a version of Holy Writ that was authorized by the renowned King James of England, who was a distant son of Japheth, King James was indeed a true history maker and one of the world's most controversial figures in the fields of religion and politics.

It seems as though the Old Testament biblical scene was primarily dominated by the sons of Shem and Ham. While the inter-testament and the New Testament period appear to have been dominated by the sons of Shem and Japheth. Please observe the wisdom and sovereignty of Elohim in the ordering of *Noah's family.* See, how interwoven the lives and destinies of Noah's three sons really are. The Holy Bible (KJV) is most accurate in showing the presence and participation in the plan of God by many nations. Each of these nations have originated from the original seventy (70) which came forth from the loins of Shem, Ham, and Japheth. These very same nations intermarried with one another and fought wars against each other. While having the same place of origin, it really doesn't compute. We must remember that the Holy Scriptures is a divine book inspired by the Spirit of Truth. Yes, the Holy Scriptures, from Genesis to Revelation, is also the Constitution of the Kingdom of God! It was the Creator-King, the Almighty, King of kings, and the Lord of lords, who gave the decree.

As to each of Noah's sons' accomplishments and their descendants' contributions to human civilization yet to come. The Divine Library or Holy Bible records historical events and figures; yet it is much more than a history book. In ignorance, many have denied such facts, believing that there was no mention of blacks in the Bible. Some believe it is not relevant or necessary to discuss such a subject. However, the Holy Scriptures are not silent or vague on the topic of black people, who are descendants of Ham and quite possibly Shem. The Scriptures do not speak of more than one race; rather it speaks loud and clear that there is only one race called *human.* Scientifically, the human race is known as homo sapiens, meaning *the primate species to which modern humans belong* (Oxford University Press). The origin of the word is Latin, which means "wise man."

As stated before, the insight gleaned through this investigation taps into the dazzling flow and light of the wisdom of God. Elohim's wisdom is far superior to anything earthly or human. The human race consists of many different hues, shades, and colors that demonstrate the beauty of Elohim's glory. The Constitution of the Kingdom has on record, throughout its sacred writ, individuals both male and female who are descendants of Ham. Listed below are (10) descendants of Ham, five (5) from the Old Testament and five (5) from the New

Testament. The student should know there are many others in the Holy Bible that descended from Ham.

Names	Scripture
Asenath, wife of Joseph	Genesis 10:6, 41:45
Abimilech	Genesis 10:17, Joshua 9:1, 3, 7 Judges 8:31, 9:1-6
Uriah, the Hittite	Genesis 10:15, 2 Samuel 11:1-27
Cushi	2 Samuel 18:21-33
Ebed-Melech	Jeremiah 38:7-13, 39:15-18
Simon of Cyrene	Matthew 27:32, Mark 15:21, Luke 23:26
Simeon called Niger	Acts 13:1
Lucius of Cyrene	Acts 13:1
Ethiopian Eunuch	Acts 8:26-39
Queen Candace	Acts 8:27

This concludes our listing of the numerous biblical characters that were present during the days of ancient Israel and the first century of the Church. There are extra biblical sources that recognize other male and female Bible characters as being of Hamitic origin. Once more, there was close interaction, intermarrying, and religious acceptance among descendants of Shem and Ham.

Later, the same type of interaction, intermarrying, and religious acceptance occurred between descendants of Shem and Japheth. Those of Semitic origin that kept hold of the traditions of Judaism emerged out of the southern Kingdom of Judah. That was a fulfillment of the LORD's prophetic word. Speaking from a geopolitical and geostrategic standpoint, it was Shem and Ham from the early beginnings of the East.

In the West, it was Shem and Japheth chiefly during the Roman occupation of Palestine during the time of Christ. Looking at the same scenario from a viewpoint of civilization, it seems as though it were descendants of Shem and Ham that reopened humankind from the East. Remembering the east is the direction of the rising sun, peering westward, the descendants of Shem and Japheth have truly expanded civilization from then until now. We should note that west is the direction of the setting sun. All of these human events on the world's stage mirror the glory of God, who watches over all things in heaven and earth. Elohim's glory will be seen by all flesh at the closing of human civilization as we know it. Then the Age of Fallen Man shall come to an end followed by the Golden Age of the Sons of God in the New Jerusalem!

The FTL Layout

The Genesis Report, chapter 10, verse 20 states the following: *"These are the sons of Ham, after their **families**, after their **tongues**, in their **nations**."* The report concludes that each of the three brothers, their children, and their descendants did not disperse properly as it would please the will of Elohim. The Tower of Babel incident served as a major catalyst for dispersion. The descendants of Shem settled in and around modern-day Arabia, parts of Asia, and India. Descendants of Japheth migrated toward the Mediterranean Sea, covering Europe and some of Asia. Ham's descendants settled all of Africa and a vast majority of the continent of Asia. Genesis 9:19 states that this was part of the LORD's original intent for *Noah's family*. Imagine families of Hamitic people with various languages and dialects gathering together in certain geographical locations. Those people or nations began to develop what we would call *culture*. One can be sure that specific customs, traditions, or peculiar ways of doing things began to appear. Most certainly, the lay of the land did help to shape these ancient people. That too was under the auspices of an all-powerful God. We have come to the end of our investigation of Noah's son, Ham.

Our search has uncovered evidence revealing the powerful epic story of *Noah's family,* which is the story of the human race and how it was successfully continued through eight souls who walked off an ark of gopher wood. During the stillness of an old preacher's home life, we witnessed his human frailty being at the ripe old age of six hundred years plus. The head of the family planted a vineyard, got drunk, naked, and finally, disrespected by one of his sons. Noah pronounced a curse on one of his grandchildren. Later, in the land of Shinar, a construction boom took place while the people of that day were under the influence of the spirit of Religion and Politics. Their goal was to build a city (politics) and a tower (religion) to make a name for themselves in the earth. Once more, the fires of human rebellion were ignited.

CHAPTER 4
Japheth: The Thinking Man

Genesis Report, chapter 9, verses 18 (a), 19, emphatically declare: *"And the sons of Noah **(the whole human race)**, that went forth of the ark, were Shem, and Ham, and Japheth . . . These are the three sons of Noah; and of them was the whole earth overspread."* After that statement, the Genesis Report records the sequence of events that transpired at the tent of Noah, the patriarch and governor of the earth. It resulted terribly for the family of man but not too difficult for Elohim to work out. Shem and Japheth acted properly and used wisdom coupled with respect to rectify a bad situation. Such actions by man always leave room for the King of glory to step in and restore things damaged by human error. So Shem, *the blessed one,* and Japheth, *the thinking man,* did act responsibly toward their father in a moment of dire circumstances. They demonstrated honor by taking a garment and laying it upon their shoulders, and going backward, covering their father's nakedness.

Japheth is listed as the third son of Noah and brother to Shem and Ham. Japheth's name has such meanings as "fair, bright, extender, expansion, and enlarge (consider explorer)." The Strong's Concordance defines Japheth as *Yepheth* (3315) meaning "opened." It has in mind from a root word the picture of an opened mouth suggesting open to deception or being gullible. One should consider if there is some type of relation between an opened mouth, being gullible or susceptible to deception and that of the mental quest that philosophers sometime engage upon. If we conduct a systematic comparison of the three brothers' names, they will line up accordingly. Shem's name declares he will be great and have notoriety. Ham's name expresses his strong physical characteristics and his ability to operate efficiently in the physical realm. Japheth's name speaks of enlarging, constantly widening in the earth from their place of origin. His descendants would conduct the same kind of expansion throughout the world. Expansion would be one of their great achievements. The annals of human history do chronicle the great feats of the sons of Japheth. We have chosen for the sake of our investigative study to identify Japheth as "the thinking man."

Right away, the famous sculpture known as *The Thinker* should come to mind. This magnificent bronze sculpture was the artistic work of French sculptor (Francois) Aguste Rene' (1840-1917), who is a distant son of Japheth. All praises to the Most High God for his infinite wisdom in the ordering of a diverse and vast human population. I believe this great sculptor epitomizes the scholarly work done by Dr. Custance. He refers to Japheth as the philosopher. As you know, philosophy cannot be formulated without the use of thought or faculty of mind. *Wilmington's Guide to the Bible,* p. 12 lists Japheth's contribution to human civilization as being the application of philosophy and the development of the scientific method. He is essentially responsible for man's mental well-being. The two processes formerly stated require mental exertion or what one might call thinking. Before moving on let us review an earlier topic of interest.

The Genesis Report has on record that Elohim assigned *Noah's family* with the monolithic task of Project Earth which entailed the renewal of the dominion mandate. Noah had executive responsibility as for as reestablishing law and order on the earth. Shem would be responsible for the spiritual aspect of Project Earth. Ham's responsibility to mankind was the physical component of Project Earth. Leaving to the Japheth the mental and intellectual portion of Project Earth. He was sort like the International Director of Philosophy and Mental Health on behalf of humanity. The Divine Constitution reads in 1 Corinthians 1:22-24, as written by the great Apostle Paul, who was a distant descendant of Shem, saying, *"For the Jews require a sign, and the Greeks seek after wisdom: But we preach Christ crucified, unto the Jews as stumbling block, and unto the Greeks foolishness; But unto them which are called, both Jews and Greeks, Christ the power of God, and the wisdom of God."*

The Paraclete or Holy Spirit gave Paul insight into the wisdom of God as it pertains to salvation and his dealings with the nations. The apostle points out that Jews, who were his own people, sought fervently after signs and wonders. Please note the wisdom in this observation. The Jews or Israel, in their excessive need for a sign, were they not simply displaying the dominant characteristics of their ancient progenitor, Shem? A person gifted by God for the express purpose of worshipping his majesty and glory would be more inclined toward being spiritual rather than a mental propensity or a physical one. They might even lean toward pursuing signs and wonders as opposed to philosophy, which is the love of wisdom. Genesis Report, chapter 10 shows that the progenitor of the Greeks is none other than Japheth, the philosopher.

There is nothing racist or prejudicial about what the Apostle Paul has written. It is the wisdom of God being disclosed to mankind. Not only is Japheth the thinking man, but he is an absorber of sorts. If one is by creative design an *extender, expander,* or *explorer,* that person would have to be of necessity absorbate.

An *absorber* would take in, ingest, assimilate, possess, or adopt whatever might be in their path. Assimilation is another distinct aspect of Japheth, the Philosopher's capabilities. His descendant-nations are also, gifted with that ability to assimilate the ideas and cultures of other nations. By taking a quick glance at the footsteps of Japheth's children in the sands of time, you will see, for certain, historical evidence of them absorbing or assimilating people, places, and a plethora of things in their path. The thinking man correlates with the order that Elohim formed the first man, Adam. Genesis Report, chapter 2, verse 7 states that the physical part of man was formed first. This act connects with Ham, who is responsible for man's physical well-being. Next Elohim breathes into the empty dust-shell and man was alive. This act of giving man the breath of life connects with Shem, who was appointed to provide for man's spiritual life. After breathing the breath of life into a lifeless physical form, man became a living soul. This final act points directly to Japheth, whose divine assignment is to contribute to man's mental well-being. We must get it into our spirits and allow our minds to be renewed to the reality that the first man was three dimensional in existence. Yes, Adam was the original worshiper, the first inventor, and he was also the original philosopher (a lover of wisdom) or thinking man.

Adam with his spirit could instantly connect and commune with the Spirit of God, and with his body, he made contact with the physical world. Lastly, Adam, through his soul, which was the seat of his intellect, emotions, and will, could be both spiritual and natural. Adam, before his fall, did not know sin nor did he know good and evil.

He only knew his Creator intimately walking with him in the cool of the day. Elohim intended for the human soul to be under the control of our spirit. Because the latent powers of the soul can be expressed mentally or through the human psyche. I am confident that mankind's mental (soulish) powers are tremendous in potential, which is why they have sovereignly been limited due to man's fallen nature. However, "the thinking man's" gift, which is possessed by the descendants of Japheth, appears to have the capacity to evolve, increase, and develop gradually over a span of time. This gift adapts well with the destiny that Noah, the patriarch declared over his son Japheth.

Their historical path has included expansion, extension, and such an enlargement that they have extended well beyond their place of origin. These are the actions of a philosopher, an individual who might ask why or why not. The late Senator Edward Kennedy quoted a similar phrase from a poem at his brother Robert Kennedy's funeral. Both of the great and noble Americans are of Irish descent and descend from Japheth.

Seven Plus Seven

Noah's prophetic pronouncement over Japheth and Shem sounded forth in this manner, *"God shall **enlarge** Japheth, and he shall dwell in the tents of Shem"* (Genesis 9:27). The Table of Nations Population Authority (TNPA) affirms in the Genesis Report, chapter 10, verses 1-4: *"Now these are the generations of the sons of Noah, Shem, Ham, and Japheth: an unto them were sons born after the flood."* It is clear at this point in time that Project Earth is under way and the offspring of Noah's sons are fully involved in various degrees and times. The report goes on to read as follows: *"The sons of Japheth; **(1) Gomer**, and **(2) Magog**, and **(3) Madai**, and **(4) Javan**, **(5) Tubal**, **(6) Meshech**, and **(7) Tiras**, And the sons of **Gomer;** **(8) Ashkenaz**, and **(9) Riphath**, and **(10) Togarmah**. And the sons **Javan;** **(11) Elishah**, and **(12) Tarshish**, **(13) Kittim**, and **(14) Dodanim"*** (Genesis 10:2-4).

Any student or investigator of truth should know that the Holy Scriptures are filled with many spiritual principles that are logical and vastly superior to human logic and reasoning. These principles are divine in origin, spiritual in nature, and are reflective of the Kingdom of heaven which is the first and original government in the universe. The Kingdom of God is not experienced through our five senses (sight, smell, sound, touch, and taste) rather righteousness, peace, and joy in the Holy Ghost. This same kingdom can be entered into here on earth. All that Elohim has done, from the sending of his only begotten Son to the promise of the Father, has been about the return of the Spirit of God on earth.

This same Spirit of God was poured out on one hundred and twenty (120) expectant believers in the palatial City of Jerusalem. The nation of Israel was politically under the vassal hegemony of the Roman Empire, who were for the most part descendants of Japheth. To fully understand the *Noah's family* revelation, a student must view it from a Kingdom perspective that is from heaven to earth and not earth to heaven or earth to earth. Any of those views simply amount to plain old earthly wisdom. Kingdom citizens should measure and weigh all fresh revelation in such a way. Inside the Kingdom of God, the principle is that the first shall be last and the last shall be first. This particular Kingdom principle can be easily seen in all of the heavenly Father's dealings with mankind. A diligent search from Genesis to Revelation will confirm whether it is factual or not. God, the Father, whose name is pronounced Yahweh, Yahveh or Yehovah, is the universal Monarch and Creator of all things in heaven and earth. It is he who has ordained the number of nations that Noah's sons would contribute to the seventy (70) nations. It was not placed on a ballot or referendum; as a matter of fact, the democratic process was not involved in any way whatsoever.

The Almighty chose Ham to make a contribution of thirty (30) nations and thereby found the earliest known civilizations. It was the King of glory who appointed twenty-six (26) nations to Shem and gave him a name above the name of his two brothers. He foreknew that Shem was the son that Israel would emerge from and ultimately provide passage for his Son to enter the earth and intervene in human history. He called forth fourteen (14) nations from the loins of Japheth for a divine purpose to be revealed after the birth of Christ. Elohim also, foreknew that the great and vast Western civilization would rise upon the earth through Noah's son Japheth, the philosopher. It would be the Western civilization that would serve as a vehicle conveying the Good News of the Kingdom to the rest of the world. Japheth's posterity through the roomy Western civilization would sway the world from the birth of Christ to this present age. It is the Western powers of this present world that are dominant in comparison to the former dominance of Eastern civilizations. The former luster of ancient Eastern superpowers has faded away under the dust and ashes of time. These very same Western powers are descendants of Japheth, *the thinking man.*

East Versus West

Since the rising of the sun in the east and its setting in the West, there has always been some type of contrast between the two directions. This geographical divide has everything to do with Noah's three sons. Most researchers, archaeologists, and anthropologists will agree that human civilization arose out of the east and spread west which is the path of our brightest star in the heavens, the sun. In addition, we can add that human civilization or the age of man will one day come to an end.

Whether it is what we call the Far East or Middle East, there has been a type of perpetual rivalry. The conflict is reminiscent of a high school football competition or a collegiate one in any sport. Did not the great Roman Empire, which arose from among the sons of Japheth, have conflict? Yes! Rome, during its declining years, eventually divided into an eastern and western empire. That decline was followed by the Crusades that also reflected this ancient rivalry and struggle of east versus west. The so-called Christian armies of Europe (West) were sent to fight and free Jerusalem from the hands of Moslem (East) forces. Once again, east opposed west on the field of battle, having both sides locked into mortal conflict to the death. In the American frontier, two great railroad companies met at Promontory, Utah, thus connecting eastern resources with western expansion. What a combination?

Post-World War II saw a great city divided into East and West Berlin. Shortly after that, the Cold War commenced between two superpowers, the United States and the USSR. There were often political showdowns and military standoffs between the USSR-East and the US-West. A sustained Cold War kept the world perpetually on the brink of war. *It appears that as far as the human race is concern World War III will always be in the shadows and unfortunately could become a reality in our approaching future.* It is our base nature and an inclination toward the dark side of reality that allows us keep the ominous threat of a third world war in the shadows of our consciousness. For the longest time, there has been a cultural conflict between the East and West. It has pitted ancient, Oriental traditions against Western technology and brash new ideas.

East versus West has at other times been a clash of philosophical views, to say the least. *In some ways, the East represents where human civilization has been, while the West boasts of where civilization is going.* The Old Testament sustains that it was Shem and

Ham's descendants that help to mold Eastern civilization. The New Testament Scriptures support that Shem and Japheth have shaped Western civilization, thereby closing out the biblical canon. Even today, cultures and ideologies clash on the field of battle and public debate. There has been an East-versus-West slant in the global war on terrorism. It is a clash of ancient cultures involving *Noah's family* engaged in a colossal conflict with each other. The Muslim extremists believe they represent Allah and the East, while the majority of the Western powers stand for democracy and Western ideologies.

The King of glory revealed himself in human form through the life and presence of Jesus Christ, who is also, known as, Yeshua HaMashiach. By, the wisdom of the God, Christ entered human history just as the Eastern civilization was beginning to decline and Western civilization was on the rise. In a sense, Christ was born at the very center of human civilization.

The Architects of the West

The phenomenal Hebrew prophet and seer, Daniel, was also known as Belteshazzar and hailed from the Israelite tribe of Judah. Daniel was on a Kingdom assignment as a plenipotentiary prophet and ambassador of the Kingdom of heaven. His embassy was located in the land of Shinar, where much of human civilization began. The land of Shinar is believed to be the ancient land of Sumer which was located in Mesopotamia, the cradle of civilization. Shinar is the geographical location of the Tower of Babel. Daniel, from a human perspective, was a captive and very much a part of the seventy years of Babylonian captivity. From a divine vantage point, Daniel and his staff of friends were on site to be Kingdom representatives. An essential component of their diplomatic appointment was to stand for Elohim and his Law before an earthly ruler and his fleeting empire.

The Gospel of Matthew, chapter 11, verse 12 records the words of Christ saying, *"And from the days of John the Baptist until now the kingdom of heaven suffereth violence, and the violent take it by force."* You see the Kingdom of heaven can withstand violence, resistance, and persecution directed toward it without prevail. It is true that during Daniel and Ezekiel's prophetic ministries, the Kingdom of Israel was divided and sentenced to exile by the Righteous Judge of all the earth. Yet both prophets represented the LORD before heathen captives and a rebellious people.

Daniel is Hebrew for "God is my judge," which is exactly what the Babylonian monarch discovered about Elohim. The LORD caused King Nebuchadnezzar to have dreams that troubled his spirit, giving him a severe case of insomnia. That particular psychological episode was not a good thing for a ruler of such a vast empire or any head of state. Eventually, Daniel's gift of dreams and interpretation brought him before the king with a divine solution. Daniel had within himself a heavenly resolution for Babylon's ruler, he was there on the behalf of the King of glory. As Elohim's spokesman he was given the meaning of King Nebuchadnezzar's dream. The king saw a great image made up of different earthly materials. What an interesting point? All earthly kingdoms, governments, and political systems created by *Noah's family* have failed miserably, which has resulted in much chaos and unrest upon the earth. Thanks be to God for his everlasting Kingdom! His divine government is one of absolute perfection and totally without flaws. It is totally pure, just, and benign it is the ultimate prototype for government. Below, we offer a brief summary of Daniel's prophetic interpretation:

Body Part	Material	Meaning
Head	*Gold*	*Babylonian Empire*
Breast / Arms	*Silver*	*Medo-Persians*
Belly / Thighs	*Brass*	*Grecian Empire*
Legs / Feet	*Iron*	*Roman Empire*

Which of Noah's sons is the progenitor of Babylon and Medo-Persia? The answers have differed from source to source and scholar to scholar. However, the progenitor of the last two empires depicted in the summary is for certain Japheth. There is no doubt in that the Greeks and Romans are sons of Japheth. Genesis Report, chapter

10, verse 2 clearly states that Japheth is a son of Noah and brother to Shem and Ham. The report reads further into the immediate lineage of Japheth, stating that Japheth fathered seven sons. The two we will highlight for this portion of our knowledge quest will be Javan and Tiras. Tiras is the founder and father of Italy or the Thracians. He could quite possibly be the same to the ancient Romans. It was the Greeks and Romans who were among the key architects and chief workers of what we have come to know as Western Civilization. These two empires were allowed by Elohim, the Creator-King and Overseer of history, to expand according to his will.

Let's try and remember that the whole purpose of human history is, "His Story" which is the greatest story ever told. How an eternal Father determined to redeem mankind by sending his only begotten Son to be a Sin-Sacrifice for the entire world. Thus, freeing the human family from the enemy of all mankind, darkness, and the relentless slavery of sin. These particular sons of Japheth (Javan and Tiras) helped lay the foundations of the West as being distinct from the East. The *Encyclopedia Encarta 2004 Edition* offers the following statement:

> *"Because of the enduring influence of its ideas, ancient Greece is known as the cradle of Western civilization. In fact, Greeks invented the idea of the West as a distinct region; it was where they lived, west of the powerful civilizations of Egypt, Babylonia, and Phoenicia."*

We can be certain that Egypt and Phoenicia are Hamitic in origin. Babylonia could quite possibly be a blend of Hamitic and Semitic roots or completely Hamitic. Both the Greeks and Romans extended their geographical borders and influence throughout the known world. They did so in the manner that Noah declared prophetically over the life of their ancient progenitor, Japheth, who is the brother to Shem and Ham. Their expansion and extension upon the earth have reflected the ways and means of a philosopher.

The Greeks and Romans were nations of *"thinking men"* that absorbed peoples and lands. Greece (Javan) was first. Their civilization flourished along the Mediterranean Sea from the third millennium to the first century BC. The Greek city-states were conquered in 146 BC by the Romans. These same Romans, who were sons of Japheth, were the vassal lords over Israel as a result of their sin and disobedience. Let the student of history and truth seeker understand that no nation or kingdom can dispossess another without the divine consent of the King of glory.

During the time of John, the Baptist, it was Rome that held the known world in its sway. It was amid the season of Rome's rule that *a voice of one crying in the wilderness* sounded forth, bringing hope to the downtrodden of Israel and to all that would believe his message. The first preaching of the Gospel of the Kingdom took place under Rome's iron and clay regime. Indeed, the iron empire was just as the Prophet Daniel saw it, a kingdom of iron mixed with clay.

Even today, that is the political mixture of all forms of human government, partly strong with good intentions, but mostly weak and frail due to human nature. All forms of human governance are at best a mixture of iron and clay to include a government by one person, a few, or the many. The Gospel of Luke, chapter 2, verse 1 says it was under the reign of Caesar Augustus that the King of kings was born. All praises to the Most High God! Consider his wisdom in that Jesus Christ descended from the heaven of heavens through Noah's son, Shem. If you will recall, the meaning of Shem's name speaks of a name, greatness, and position.

Remember, Jesus or Yeshua was given a name by his heavenly Father that far exceeds the greatness or prominence of any other name born on planet Earth. The Son of God's name is the ultimate fulfillment of Shem's name. Jesus is Shem's most blessed Son and descendant, a name above all names, greater than any in the east or west. His name has not only gone down in history, his name is 'his-story'. The Son's name is superior! *Having a full understanding of this divine reality makes racism and anti-Semitism one of the greatest follies of our modern times.* His name is a strong tower and shield to be trusted in for one's salvation and victory. Still, we must point out that Caesar Augustus was a son of Japheth. It is absolutely amazing how the King of glory has kept *Noah's family* together even through their internal strife and conflicts. He kept representatives from each brother close around his eternal plans until the timely arrival of his Son. The Father marked out beforehand that Jesus would restore all things. He gave Christ the ultimate vision for the good and betterment of all humanity. His vision was to restore the Kingdom back to man, build a society of humans committed to his teachings, and establish an unbreakable covenant with his blood. The cross of Christ is the universal joint for the human race and the only place for redemption, equality, and original freedom. The sons of Japheth are in fact the architects of the West and founders of Western Civilization as authorized by the Most High God.

Democracy and Res Publica

World history verifies the accuracy of the Holy Scriptures repeatedly. Consequently, Japheth and the majority of his descendants migrated to what is now called the continent of Europe and almost a quarter of Asia. The word *democracy* stems from the Greek language. It means *demos*, which means "the people." *Kratein* means "to rule." So, a democracy is a form of government in which the people rule, as opposed to one person having sole power and authority.

Ancient Greece practiced a form of pure democracy, wherein only the eligible among the citizenry could take part in governing. Their political assemblies were called *Ecclesia,* which means "an assembly of called-out ones." These assemblies consisted of as much as 500 people, mostly free men, for there were certain restrictions on who could participate and be involved in the matters of government. The Gospel of Matthew, chapter 16, verse 18 records a powerful, prophetic declaration by Jesus just as they were entering the coasts of Caesarea Philippi. This is first mentioning of the word *church.* The Greek word *ecclesia* is translated into the English word Church.

Please note that the original text of the New Testament was written in Greek and Aramaic.

Sharing the Greek language with the world is another dynamic contribution to civilization by one of Japheth's descendants. I believe Jesus Christ, who is the King of glory manifested in human form chose purposely to disclose the mystery of the Church at that precise time. As he spoke to his apostles about the Church that he was going build and how it would withstand death and the forces of darkness. Christ was well aware of the Caesar that ruled an earthly empire from the City of Rome and the *ecclesia* that assisted him with the affairs of state. The Roman Senate was Caesar's church or *ecclesia*, which helped him to govern the empire. What a showdown! The Caesar who occupied the throne at that time had his own church for the fulfillment of his own selfish desires. Jesus Christ, the savior of the world informed his apostolic staff that he would build a Church that would have no restrictions – a Church that would include Jew (Shem) and Gentile (Japheth), male and female, bond or free. The heavenly Father is awesome in his use of wisdom and power.

Today, modern democracies of the West do not practice pure democracy but a more representative form of government. The philosophers of Greece facilitated to shape the political views and ideologies of all future democracies. Later in 146 BC, Roman conquerors defeated the Greek city-states. Afterwards, the Romans adopted or shall we say absorbed much of the Greek customs, ideas, and practices. Greek concepts and culture are also known as Hellenism. Indeed, Hellenistic views did shape the foundations and way of life of the ancient Romans. In many regards, they built upon what the Greeks had already established.

The language of the Romans was Latin, which was very different from Greek. Our English word for republic has its roots in Latin. The ancient Romans developed their own political system, which they called *res publica*, literally "the public thing." It was based upon the concept that sovereignty resides in the people, who would elect representatives to govern on their behalf. Rome started out being ruled by kings until the last of the seven kings had to step down from his throne. That action led to the establishment of the Roman republic; first under the rule of magistrates and other representatives elected by the people. By 30 BC, Rome was again under the power of kings and became the Roman Empire. Their great empire was immensely influenced by ancient Greece.

Democratic and republic theory are just two of the many great gifts that the sons of Japheth have bestowed upon human civilization. Both democracy and res publica emanate from the original gift of Japheth, the philosopher, *the thinking man.*

Science and Philosophy

Noah, the patriarch clearly declared over his son Japheth saying, *"God shall enlarge Japheth, and he shall dwell in the tents of Shem"* (Genesis 9:27 (a)). The enlargement, extension, and expansion capabilities of Japheth could be compared to the way a man's mind or intellect can be expanded over a period of time. Through the development of scientific method and philosophy, Japheth would truly extend his influence upon history. Descendants of Japheth would benefit the most from his original gift that was divinely granted to him for the betterment of mankind. Science and philosophy would become very effective tools in the hands of Japheth's children. I believe the very essence of the two disciplines is their unlimited potential to dilate and become wider in reach.

Japheth was appointed by Elohim to be responsible for mankind's mental well-being. Remember, Shem was gifted with the religious insights for the responsibility of man's spiritual life. Ham was given technical proficiency and thereby obligated for man's physical life. Dr. Custance suggested in his *Doorway Papers* that Japheth's gift enabled him to lay out excellent ideals which would be his chief product. He further offered that after an ideal or idea had been exhibited, Japheth was limited as far as the implementation of that particular ideal or idea. It is a limitation that does not in any form diminish the power and potential of the ideal. Such an unfortunate fact is not unusual, because each of Noah's sons had limitations on their individual gifts. Each gift had a specific limit or measure which has allowed for much success but more often resulted in failure.

Once more, we can confirm that the archives of human history hold the records of such evidence. For centuries, archeologists have studied ancient ruins and witnessed firsthand the strengths and weaknesses of Noah's sons as seen in the posterity of Shem, Ham, and Japheth. The potential of Japheth's gift empowered him to apply the religious insights of Shem with his philosophy, and theology was born to the world. Systematic Theology has blessed the world with an A-to-Z method and approach. Systematic Theology has aided mankind in understanding and being able to interpret the Holy Bible better. Japheth applied his gift of philosophy with Ham's inventiveness and technical proficiency thereby, creating technology. I am certain no one would deny that technology has been a significant component in the advancement and dominance of Western Civilization.

The King of Javan

Japheth, a son of Noah had seven (7) sons, of which Gomer had three (3) sons and Javan had four (4) sons. Javan was the fourth son of Japheth, whose future generations populated ancient Greece or Ionia. Javan had a future son that established his place in the great hall of historical achievements. He was the formidable and extremely ambitious Alexander, the Great. The prophetic Book of Daniel, chapter 8, verse 21 speaks of the King of Grecia as being the rough goat in Daniel's prophetic vision. Most scholars believe that the King of Grecia is none other than Alexander, the son of Philip of Macedonia. The King of glory used Daniel's gift of dream interpretation to reveal the dawning of the brass kingdom on the horizon of history. Alexander, at age twenty, succeeded his father Philip, who was assassinated in 336 BC. His father had succeeded in forming the Hellenic confederacy, whose primary goal was to cross the Hellespont and defeat the Medo-Persian Empire.

This very goal became Alexander's great quest and mission, which he successfully accomplished. One of the many benefits of Alexander's magnificent conquests was the spreading of the Greek language and Hellenism. This is just another splendid contribution made by the sons of Japheth for the good of humankind. On June 13, 323 BC, Alexander died from a high fever contracted six days earlier. He was thirty-two years of age! Thus, was the ending of an illustrious twelve-year military and political career by one of the most fascinating conquerors of all time. He was Alexander, the Great, the King of Javan.

The Isles of the Gentiles

We can continue to rely upon the accuracy of the Genesis Report for revelation and information. In chapter 10, verse 5 it reads as follows: *"By these were **the isles of the Gentiles** divided in their lands; every one after his tongue, after their families, in their nations."* Notice the reference to *"isles"* has an exact point to make. It makes reference to the geographical region or area that is being described. I have reviewed the report many times, and each time the Spirit of Truth reveals more wisdom and understanding. The former is essential if one is going to understand the ways and thoughts of Elohim.

Book of Wisdom, Proverbs 4:7 is a beautiful passage of scripture that sheds some light on an essential need of all men. Each narrative pertaining to Noah's sons is quite specific and not lacking in depiction. It was as if the King of glory in a direct or indirect fashion was preparing for a press conference. It was not as though the Creator of the universe would need to explain himself to mortal man.

The Book of Job is one of the five books of wisdom and considered to be the oldest book in the King James Version of the Holy Bible. The same gives an account of Job and his friends trying to interrogate and presume to know the mind of Elohim. Out of a whirlwind, the LORD began to instruct these finite men about their limited notions. He did so with infinite wisdom and knowledge that caused Job to repent or change his mind. He offers testimony in the forty-second chapter of his book.

A Press Conference with the Almighty

Nevertheless, if the Creator were to grant such an audience to mere mortals, it might proceed in the following manner:

Thomas Seeker: Your Majesty, what was a specific point that you wanted to convey in the biblical text?

The Almighty: Yes, Thomas, you have asked an excellent question.

The Almighty: First, if you will observe how I allowed Noah to declare over Shem's life that he would be blessed and Japheth would be enlarged and dwell in his tents. It shall be my presence that shall abide with all who shall enter into the tents of Shem for there I have commanded a blessing to abide forever. You see, I gave Shem tents or dwelling places in the earth that would bless all future nations of mankind. If you will note, he is the only one of the three brothers that was given tents. Because of the breaking of one of my commandments, the fifth to be exact, Noah cursed Canaan. He was Ham's youngest son and the first occupant of what you now call Palestine until I gave it to Abraham's seed because of his righteousness. Behold, the description "servant of servants shall he be unto his brethren" might sound to a carnal or natural mind to be the end or very degrading and demeaning. However, nothing could be further from the truth! Remember, I sent my Son thousands of years later in the form of a suffering Servant, and I have made mere service the standard of excellence in my Kingdom. My Son, Yeshua, taught that it was how one can become great and exemplify greatness for my sake. I appointed Japheth, son of Noah, to enlarge, extend, expand, and to be roomy upon the earth. The events that occurred at Noah's tent were of a truth the epicenter of human history. By my wisdom, I decreed that from fourteen nations, a great civilization would emerge – a civilization that would be in place at the time of my Son's birth and remain until the end of this age. In my Kingdom, which is eternal and above all the kingdoms of the earth, I can take a little, the least, or that which has been judged weak and will cause it to multiply. This I do according to my wisdom, predestinate counsel, and might. The Isles of the Gentiles were given to the sons of Japheth for a geographical designation and a mark of distinction. Other versions of my Holy Script describe Japheth's descendants as "maritime nations" or "the coastland peoples." Your earth scientists refer to a certain landmass as Europe and that particular region as the Mediterranean. During their time, I would allow Japheth's children to enlarge from Europe to the rest of the world. Indeed, this was the process that enabled Japheth to "dwell in the tents of Shem."

<u>*Thomas Seeker:*</u> *Majesty, I still don't understand! What's the point and what about the problems in the world?*

<u>*The Almighty:*</u> *Behold, I created man for communion, fellowship, and to worship me. Again, I chose Noah's immediate family and spared them my judgment of water. I blessed them to multiply and replenish the earth; it was my will. I have given the earth to man that he might subdue it and have dominion. As a human family, you are not able to resolve your differences nor reclaim Creation because of your flesh. Through my Son, Yeshua, you can do all things; apart from him, you cannot. Your history holds within it the evidence of your need for my grace and mercy.*
<u>*Thomas Seeker:*</u> *Majesty, how can we prove such things?*

<u>*The Almighty:*</u> *There will be no more questions, only believe!*

What an informative press conference with absolutely no spin as only the Almighty could give. Such a conference would be exciting, riveting, and exhilarating, with compelling answers coming straight from the mouth of Elohim. He is the source of all Truth, Light, and Love in the universe.

More Exculpatory Evidence

Before reading this section or topic, the student would be wise to keep in mind that *Noah's family* are the makers of history. From ancient times to this present day, the descendants of Noah's three sons have for centuries interacted upon the earth. John L. Johnson (a son of Ham / Shem) in his book *The Black Biblical Heritage* – p. 12 identifies Japheth as the father of Gentile nations. He further adds that in most revised Bibles, the word Gentile, in relation to Japheth, has been removed. In light of such a statement, we remain aware that Elohim is the source of all truth and he is absolutely pure and just. Now concerning world dominion, the Almighty, who is the very embodiment of love, has granted each of Noah's sons a span or period of time for world domination. Each of their seasons of rule would end rather abruptly due to sin and disobedience.

Still another source, *Wilmington's Guide to the Bible* – p. 33 cites renowned German theologian Eric Sauer (a son of Japheth). He writes: "With Nimrod began, with Hannibal ended the drama of Hamitic World Empire, and Rome's brilliant victory sealed conclusively the establishment of the world-rule of the Japhetic race. 'Let Canaan be his servant' – this it is which stands as written, as with letters of fire, over the battlefield of Zama." So, it is written in *Dawn of World Redemption* (p. 80). There is nothing negative nor racist about Mr. Sauer's statement, just as there nothing racist or negative about Mr. Johnson's statement. Both statements are strongly supported by historical evidence, even biblical history. *Whenever secular and sacred history flow parallel to each other we call this affect the Mesopotamia Method.*

The eternal Father, who is the Father of all living things by right of Creation, has permitted human events to unfold according to his will and way. Deep within the Father's mind, he had already purposed to send his only begotten Son as a sacrifice for mankind.

And he came during *the times of the Gentiles,* that is when the Roman Empire held world dominion. This dominion was granted him by the sovereignty of God only for a season. The *Microsoft – Encarta Encyclopedia Standard 2004 Edition* (listed under Diplomacy) said this about Rome: *"Rome issued commands; it did not negotiate." And so, this was the spirit and attitude of the Roman Empire.* This same Roman spirit of commanding other nations permeates many Western powers of today.

Yet the Father chose the time of the Romans to send Jesus for the whole world. He was manifested to destroy the works of the devil at a time when Japheth's children had extended their influence from the Isles of the Gentiles to the dusty roads of Palestine. Elohim sent him just in time; so that he might reveal to Israel and all nations (Noah's Family) the heavenly Father. For only the Son could adequately reveal the Father.

Luke 21:24

Purposely, we will move on from the origin of the geographical location of Japheth and his children, the Isles of the Gentiles. To fully understand *the times of the Gentiles,* a student must carefully study Luke's account of Christ's prophetic discourse of what will transpire with the temple, Jerusalem, and the last days. Jesus revealed to his disciples that the beautifully adorned temple would be destroyed and Jerusalem would be trodden under the feet of the Gentiles until *the times of Gentiles be fulfilled.* He spoke of signs in the heavens and distress upon the earth. This description is quite gloomy and bleak, with the only hope being our hope of glory, Jesus Christ. All praises to the Most High God!

The Governor of the nations makes reference to *the times of the Gentiles.* Christ's reference to the Gentiles had something to do with a measure of time or a specific period of time in human history. One can be certain that Elohim, from the beginning of Creation to the seventh day, has predetermined every season and purpose within the course of history. It is as if the Almighty had a divine planner filled with detailed dates, events, and births of key individuals. Special occurrences have already been marked beforehand. The birth of his Son has been the most anticipated and significant event in all of human history. Elohim revealed to the Prophet Daniel, *the times of the Gentiles.*

Beginning possibly as early as the rise of the Brass Kingdom, which was the Greek or Grecian Empire, the LORD allowed Daniel to see the rise of Japhetic nations on the world stage.

These events did signify the coming of the King and his kingdom. After Pentecost, the Holy Ghost revealed to Paul, who was the apostle to the Gentiles, divine insight into a great mystery. Paul, the emissary of the King of glory writes in his Letter to Romans, chapter 11, verse 25: *"For I would not, brethren, that ye should be ignorant of this mystery, lest ye should be wise in your own conceits; that blindness in part is happened to Israel, until **the fullness of the Gentiles** be come in."* Paul's apostleship was bestowed upon him by God through Christ. He was a son of Shem representing the Kingdom of Elohim to the saints at Rome. It was his desire that the church planted there would be not ignorant concerning this particular aspect of God's eternal plan. The nation of Israel, whose descent is from Shem was divinely chosen by God, the Father to be custodians of his Law. Secondly, Israel was formed to facilitate the arrival of the Son of God and thirdly, Israel was to be a blessing to other nations and a sort of prototype for them to follow. Finally, the formation of Israel is a beautiful example of divine election. Paul writes that in this limited period of time, his home nation, Israel, would be blinded because of their unbelief in the Messiah. He informs his readers clearly that this was done so, that the season of great grace might be extended to the Gentile (sons of Japheth) world.

Yes, Jesus Christ or Yeshua Hamashiach was born during *the times of the Gentiles.* Christ chose twelve men as disciples, who later became his apostles during *the times of the Gentiles.* Saul of Tarsus, who later became Paul, was converted during *the times of the Gentiles* on the famed road to Damascus. All of these things took place at the right time according to the counsel and will of

God. It was the time period for the sons of Japheth to be dominant as world powers. In the year 2010 until 2021, we are in the times of the Gentiles. I was born in AD 1965 or "in the year of our LORD." In fact, the discovery and founding of America was all done during *the times of the Gentiles.* Jesus was not revealing to those present a racial perspective, for there is only one race and that is the human race, made up of many nations. Jesus was disclosing to the twelve and others that the last days would occur during a time frame in world history – a time that the sons of Japheth would have world dominion.

Through our research, we have become aware of Western society's use of the birth of Christ as a dividing line. All time before the birth of Christ is considered as BC or before Christ. While time and history after the birth of Christ are AD or Anno Domini which means "in the year of LORD." If you will recall from a previous section, it is the mighty sons of Japheth who are the founders of Western Civilization.

What began in ancient Greece and Rome has expanded to other continents to include North and South America. The Julian calendar is named after one Rome's greatest Caesars, Gaius Julius Caesar, a son of Japheth. On the Ides of March, this son of Japheth was brutally assassinated by his fellow Romans. After his assassination, all subsequent rulers of Rome were called Caesars. Other Japhetic nations adopted the same title for their rulers but with a slight derivation, i.e., Kaiser and Czar. These two titles have been used by Germans and Russians, both descended from Japheth, a son of Noah. All of these developments have taken place during *the times of the Gentiles.* The history of Western Civilization can be divided into the following time periods:

Western Civilization
Ancient times from 3000 BC to 400 AD
Medieval times from 400 AD 1500 AD
Modern times from 1500 AD to the present

I resolve that *the times of the Gentiles* Jesus spoke of were the ancient, medieval, and modern times of mankind. These distinct time periods do classify and summarize the epoch of Western Civilization as established by the descendants of Japheth, a son of Noah.

Extension by Explorers and Expansionists

Noah declared that Elohim would enlarge Japheth significantly and that he would dwell in tents possessed by Shem. Japheth did live up to his name. The meaning of his name prophesied of the destiny that the King of glory appointed to him. His ability *"to become roomy, enlarge, extend, expand"* has caused his descendants to emerge as the greatest "expansionists of all time." This action was a definite part of God's plan from the very beginning. Japheth was ordained by Elohim to close out this present age of mankind, as were his brothers. Shem and Ham were appointed to found and enlighten human civilization right from the start.

Noah's three sons were appointed by the sovereignty of God, and nothing in heaven or earth, real or imagined, or anything could overturn his ruling. His sovereignty reflects his wisdom, perfection, and divine pattern in all things. By the use of science and philosophy, the sons of Japheth have extended their influence throughout time. They have expanded into previously occupied lands explored uncharted regions on land, the oceans, and finally space. Expansion and exploration are a part of Japheth's contribution to the age of mankind. He extended from the isles of the Mediterranean region to the eastern shores of North America. This trek began with the thinkers and philosophers on a small island, to become scientists and political theorists of a continent, to the ships, armadas, and maiden voyages of great explorers. To the early and bold expansionists of colonial America, who embraced the tenets of *Manifest Destiny.*

The phrase was first coined by American journalist and diplomat John Louis O'Sullivan, who wrote an editorial supporting the annexation of Texas. Japheth's descendants have continued a journey that began in the east. The successions that have taken place between

Shem, Ham, and Japheth over the course of time resemble the kinetic motion of relay runners, passing the baton in a close race to the finish line. The *times of the Gentiles* was the beginning of Japheth's time to grasp the baton of world leadership. Here is a manifest of courageous explorers who have descended from Japheth, the philosopher. He is the father of all Caucasian people, Japheth, the thinking man.

- Gaius Julius Caesar (58-52 BC) conquered and explored most of Western Europe and part of Britain.
- Eric, the Red (982-986 BC) explored and colonized the southwest coast of Greenland.
- Leif Eriksson (about AD 1000) explored Vinland, identified as the coast of Labrador, of Newfoundland Island, of Nova Scotia, and New England.
- Marco Polo (AD 1271-1295) traveled through Central Asia, India, China, and Malay Archipelago.
- Christopher Columbus (AD 1492-1504) explored America and established colonies during four voyages across the Atlantic.
- Vasco da Gama (AD 1497-1498) sailed around Cape of Good Hope to Malindi on the coast of Africa and then across the Indian Ocean to Calicut, India.
- Amerigo Vespucci (AD 1497-1502) sailed through the Caribbean Sea along the coast of South America. The German geographer Martin Waldseemuller published his accounts and suggested that the New World be named America. How about that? The United States of America owes its name to an Italian-born explorer.
- Francisco Pizarro (AD 1523-1535) explored the west coast of South America and conquered Peru.
- Even modern explorers, Neil A. Armstrong and Edwin E. Aldrin, Jr. (AD 1969) were the first persons to land on the moon. *"Houston, Tranquility Base Here. The Eagle has landed."*

The list goes on and on! There are far too many to enumerate. These are the sons of Japheth, who have originated from various European nations like Norway, Iceland, Portugal, Italy, Spain, England, the Netherlands, France, Denmark, Scotland, Ireland, Germany, Wales, British India, New Zealand, and Sweden. Japheth, the philosopher, thinker, and absorber of sorts has endeavored diligently and sometimes relentlessly in an effort to extend the borders of human civilization.

Many conquered peoples, nations, and cultures have been absorbed or assimilated by Japheth's children. All praises to Most High God! Amidst all of the extending, exploring, and expanding, the sons of Japheth have assumed the responsibility of helping to spread the Word of God, starting with the Gutenberg press to the completion of the biblical canon. The heavenly Father, through his infinite wisdom, has allowed the Gospel of the Kingdom to travel on the back of Western Civilization. Upon its wings of progress although sometimes controversial the Almighty sent his Word forth for the salvation of the whole world.

The *times of the Gentiles* has been an exciting time in human history for the glory of the LORD shall be seen by all flesh. The *times of the Gentiles* have been an era of philosophy, great thoughts, sculpture, exploration, and expansion, but most of all, the Word of God has been taken to the nations.

Families, Tongues, and Land

We must not be mistaken. Just as Africa is known as the land of Ham and Asia that of Shem, so it is that Europe is predominantly the land of Japheth. What are the things that have risen out of the soil of Europe? Peasant farmers, classes of nobleman, knights of a round table, castes of craftsmen, priestly orders, schools of philosophers, potentates, and royal dynasties and Slavic tongues – Gaelic, Old English, good Greek, old Latin, and fabulous French. Also, epic stories of Norsemen, bagpipes of Scotland, Welshman, Swedes, and Danes, as well as tales of Olympus, Jupiter, and Norse mythology! All these amazing things emerged from the Isles of the Gentiles.

CHAPTER 5
The Sons of Noah

Shem, Ham, and Japheth were quite possibly three of the most important men upon planet Earth after the Great Flood. From their loins would emerge human civilization once more. These men were the progenitors of a new humanity; one in which they would live on through their descendants. Elohim appointed to Shem position and the gift of spirituality for the good of humanity. He gave to Ham great physical ability and the gift of technique for civilization's good. And to Japheth he allotted extensive action and the gift of philosophy for all of mankind.

Genesis Report, chapter 9, verses 18-20 gives a detailed account of some serious family drama ending with a prophetic declaration. Since the Great Flood, the receding of the waters, and a domestic scene at Noah's tent, human history has been written and acted out by the collective efforts of the descendants of Noah's three sons. Noah was chosen by Elohim to build an ark for the salvation of man, but only his immediate family were recipients. Many generations later Elohim, the Father sent Jesus for the purpose of salvation and redemption of Noah's broader family, which is the entire human race. Only the Son of God can save man from sin and death. Jesus Christ can heal, deliver, and set the captives free.

Blessed is the name of the LORD, for it is he who governs and oversees history determining the endless bounds of the flow of time. He chose Jesus to capture, captivity and give gifts unto men. Only Jesus could deliver the human race from the final judgment of the Father's fearful wrath. The LORD chose Shem to be the *comfort person* to the rest of the family of man. Through Shem, Abraham was to separate for a season and enter into a land that was not his at the time. Israel and Ishmael are sons of Shem. Since the end of World War II, they have gained the world's center of attention and contention. Blessed be the LORD God of Shem, for he did not stop there!

He chose Ham's descendants to manifest some of the most awesome and remarkable feats of strength coupled with great technical proficiency. Thousands of inventions can be directly attributed to the sons of Ham. Yet the LORD God did not stop there! He chose Japheth, the thinking man, to share with world savvy political ideas, isms, and systems. His descendants are the originators of political theory and reform, often attempting to manage some of the international conflicts.

Alas, the rising sun does so swiftly from its encampment in the east. Likewise, the civilization of man originated from the east and has expanded expeditiously toward the west. However, let us remember the following quote by this author. *"If there is no sunrise without the expectation of a sunset, how long would a single day last?"* Japheth was meant to expand, to extend, and to make room. The sons of Japheth have expanded mankind and civilization westward, largely through technological advances. It has been his divine destiny to do. Now are the waning days of Japheth's children, for the sun rays of time are about to cast on the edge of forever.

After this son of Noah has completed his day, there will be no more days of the sons of men, for it will be that great and terrible Day of the LORD. A day when *Noah's family*, which means all flesh shall see together the son of man's day in its fullness and glory. Finally, the nations will see what Peter, James, John, Moses, and Elias saw on the Mount of Transfiguration according to the Gospel of Matthew 17:1-9. They all witnessed Jesus transform his physical appearance as the Strong's Concordance describes, 'resplendent with divine brightness'. The psalmist wrote: *"The heavens declare the glory of God; and the firmament sheweth his handywork"* (Psalms 19:1).

After applying the Mesopotamia Method, the following statement should be contemplated:

> "Consider the earth as a prophetic time clock: Israel is the large hand and the Gentiles are the short hand. While the sons of Ham are the hash marks on the clock."

Color-struck

As a student of ethnology, I am inclined toward understanding the root cause behind mankind's obsession with skin color. Ethnology is listed by the Oxford University Press Dictionary as a noun. Some of the derivatives are *ethnologic, ethnological,* and *ethnologist.* It is defined as: "the study of the characteristics of different peoples and the differences and relationships between them."

The characteristics spoken of are physical but not limited to just the physical realm entirely. Skin color or complexion is among the various physical characteristics that a particular group or people might have. All things have a beginning and an ending, a root and a branch. This part of our investigation will be focused on primarily the root cause of this apparent human obsession over skin color.

Although the civilization of man has advanced tremendously by way of science and technology. Yet, humankind's primal nature that seized dominance after the fall of Adam, the first man is helplessly prone toward disobedience in its relationship with the Creator and his fellow man. Man's nature had become more inclined to sin against Elohim. His Adamic nature gave him a proclivity or a leaning to walk contrary to his original purpose, which was to worship God and be in constant communion and relationship with him. That is why the new birth is a prerequisite for entry into the Kingdom of God. Simply put, mankind has better toys, but overall, he is still prideful and rebellious toward the things of God, apart from receiving a new nature. Herein lies the deeply rooted problem in human nature and that is the law of sin. *It is the law of sin and death working deep within our flesh that causes us to hold onto racism.*

Whenever one might speak of human society as being *color-struck* or having a bent toward prejudice and bigotry based on skin color. We have come to an understanding that neither Shem, Ham, Japheth nor any of their descendants could be entirely blamed for creating a *color-struck* society. They all have had a hand in it to some degree. Once the train of ignorance left the station, it gained momentum and has not slowed down since. Glory be to God, it is not unstoppable, for all things are possible through Jesus Christ. Sin is the original weapon of mass destruction, death is the devil's soldier (assassin), and satan is the god of this world.

Sin has no specific racial or ethnic profile; it is a human dilemma. Sin has plagued and destroyed every branch of *Noah's family* from the tent until now. The corridors of history have been stained with the filth of racism and unrighteousness of every man toward his neighbor. Sin has no respecter of persons or any specific nation. Truthfully, speaking history records quite vividly Shemites, Hamites, and Japhetites, all falling short of the glory of Elohim. The Paraclete or Holy Spirit revealed to the Apostle Paul some very deep things about human behavior and the psyche of man. He wrote extensively on the subject in his letter to the church at Rome. He explained to fellow Kingdom citizens the blessedness of their new position in Christ and what he had delivered them from. He made it very clear to them that all men have sinned and fallen short of the glory of God and are therefore in need of redemption and restoration. He elaborates more fully in chapters 6-8 the difference between the Law and grace and how Kingdom citizens can overcome sin and walk in the newness of life. He encourages them not to allow sin to reign or be in control in their mortal bodies. He admonishes by saying: *"For the wages of sin is death; but the gift of God is eternal life through Jesus Christ our LORD"* (Romans 6:23).

In Romans 7:12, he instructs: *"Wherefore the law is holy, and the commandment holy, and just, and good."* He continues his instruction in verse 14: *"For we know that the law is spiritual but I am carnal, sold under sin."* This insight given by the Holy Spirit of God reveals very clearly why humanity has difficulty with such a beautiful thing as the diversity of skin color. By the Spirit, Paul labors in his writings as to why believers might strive to do good, but evil is present; only to find themselves doing the very thing they wished not to do. The apostle offers the following perception: *"Now then it is no more I that do it, but sin that dwelleth in me.* (vv.17) *For I know that in me (that is, in my flesh,) dwelleth no good thing; for to will is present with me; but how to perform that which is good I find not."* (vv.18)

You see the racism and vitriol is a result of the ignorance of Elohim's love for diversity and variety. Racism and vitriol are manifest through the weakness of the flesh – again it is the law of sin and death working deep in human nature. The solution is the law of the Spirit of life in Christ Jesus, making all men free from that law of darkness. *Color-struck* will always exist as long as men reject what the LORD has created and refuse to follow Christ. Racism is an evil power that has been decisively defeated at the cross of Christ. Men need only to believe, understand, and appropriate the power of the cross where it is needed.

Racism cannot be ignored! Rather it must be resisted because it has been taught but now it must be untaught. Where do we begin this righteous crusade and the much-needed moral reformation? The answer is simple we, begin at the House of Elohim (God), the very place where judgment begins.

I can recall during my years of schooling, reading from an encyclopedia on the three classifications of race. I remember reading the words: Caucasoid, Negroid, and Mongoloid. The impression it gave me is still very fresh in my mind as if it was yesterday. Something on the inside of me knew that those *classifications* were incorrect. Looking back decades later I am fully persuaded that the *classifications* were man-made insertions, unfounded views based upon earthly wisdom and not wisdom from above.

Another incident that I have remembrance of took place in my third-grade year. I asked my teacher about some Brazilian nuts that we had received during the holiday season. Her reply was quite vivid. She told me that those particular nuts were called "Negro toes." Why would this brilliant and seasoned teacher give such an answer to one of her black students? I was not offended by the remark, but for some reason, it remained with me until this day. It was as if the LORD wanted me to have such an experience for my own learning and personal journey.

While conducting research for the first edition of Noah's Family. I came across some information by way of the Internet that stated that the Egyptians, (sons of Ham) engaged in some discriminative practices. Lighter-skinned Egyptians claimed that darker-skinned Egyptians were of more evil intent, while on the other hand, darker-skinned Egyptians asserted that the lighter-skinned Egyptians were more prone to evil behavior. During my lifetime I can recall hearing those same assertions within the African American community. Elsewhere in the world on the continent of Europe, a certain ideology emerged that the fairer or lighter one's complexion was the more intelligent a person was considered to be. Cranial size and development were used to measure or speculate one's intelligence. The darker a person's skin was, the less intelligent he was considered.

On the continent of Asia, it has been said among the people of India that lighter skin made one closer to the divine and darker-skinned ones further from the divine. Blacks in America have, since the days of slavery, had a diversity of skin complexions and tones. Miscegenation and intermarrying were key factors contributing to the different hues among African slaves. Many African Americans have mistreated and abused one another for decades because of skin complexion. In the historical past of American slavery, it was a well-known fact that fairer-skinned slaves were treated better than darker-skinned slaves. This very fact could be evidence of the underlying problem that Western civilization has with skin color. We should remember that it was probably white slave owners and overseers who implemented the unfair attitude toward slaves that were not in their favor. This was of course by design and the policy of those who wanted to preserve slavery as an institution. Their treatment toward slaves was deliberate and strategic. Its effectiveness is evident today as a lasting legacy of shame and injustice. For the slaves, it kept them divided and not united against their oppressors.

Love has no specific color; for all people of the earth seek and require it for existence. Most importantly, God is Love! Each human society has embraced its own strange preferences and idiosyncrasies; for example, the preferred tiny feet of the Orient, the elongated necks of Africa, and the West's ultra-thin beauty requirements. Being *color-struck* or too color conscious is simply a work of the flesh. Human nature or the flesh is just too open for the force of sin to perpetuate its downward spiral away from the presence of God. My father whom I loved dearly would often say to me, "Man grows wiser but weaker with each generation."

CONCLUSION

The impact from the Tower of Babel incident has been felt by the generations of humans that have descended from Shem, Ham, and Japheth. Mankind has acquired numerous cultural refinements, achieved a plethora of educational pursuits, and made a great many technological advancements. Yet, the babble that caused humanity to be further scattered over the earth has not ceased to exist. Religion and Politics continue to move civilization forward one step, then backward two or three steps.

An ancient unification of nations happened on the fertile plains of Shinar, which is located in Mesopotamia. Plans were devised for building a city and tower so that *Noah's family* could have a name upon the earth. Once more an act of treason and sedition against the King of glory takes place. It seems as though human beings insist on trying to have a viable future apart from the one who created them.

Even today, the United Nations diligently attempts to make the world better and more peaceful. Countless men and women have lived and died since the flood of Noah's generation. We, the people have really tried to make the world better attaining only a minimal success but nothing long lasting. However, as human beings, we should strive to leave the world just a little brighter than when we found it. After all, we were all created in the image of God.

Hatred, bigotry, and extreme variances will continue to be major obstacles to harmony. We were created to be powerful and have dominion on earth but not apart from the will of God.

Noah's family wrestles with the will of a loving Father, who desires the best for his creation. It is this struggle of will deep within the soul of man that does not allow him to be totally free nor can he allow his fellow man to be free.

At the very core of our intellect, emotions and will, a colossal conflict is being waged between our best and the worst. We can choose to do good or evil, stand for justice or injustice! Have we as an intelligent species really made substantial progress? For centuries, we have built monuments for our own self interests. From ziggurats, to pyramids, great cities with walls, hanging gardens, magnificent libraries, halls of justice, peace accords, and thousands of magnificent achievements.

Where is the place that one can be free and let others be free? Where is the place that we can look back on history and weep but still have joy? Where is the place that great and small can enjoy an equal standing? Where is the place that the frail teeming masses of humanity can be blessed and truly prosperous?

That place is the greatest place in human history, on the outskirts of the city of David. It is the place where Shem's greatest Son was crucified and later glorified. That place was and still is the cross of Jesus Christ. It is through the death of Christ that his Kingdom is released, a Church built for Jew and Gentile. And a New Covenant unveiled to the entire world.